Business Intelligence

An Essential Beginner's Guide to BI, Big Data, Artificial Intelligence, Cybersecurity, Machine Learning, Data Science, Data Analytics, Data Mining, Social Media and Internet Marketing

Contents

Introduction

Hello and welcome to *Business Intelligence - An Essential Beginner's Guide to BI, Big Data, Artificial Intelligence, Cybersecurity, Machine Learning, Data Science, Data Analytics, Data Mining, Social Media and Internet Marketing.*

In this book, we are going to introduce you to the concept of business intelligence. Business intelligence is closely connected to data, and so as part of our journey, we are going to see how modern companies are using big data, together with artificial intelligence, machine learning, and pattern recognition in order to build systems of data-driven decision making.

In the modern business world, the pace of action continues to quicken. Businesses need to be able to get actionable insights from their data in order to make the right decisions to act rapidly and effectively.

After we get a handle on what business intelligence is, we will learn how it ties together with the next computer revolution (happening right before our eyes). We will discuss the use of artificial intelligence, machine learning, and pattern recognition to retrieve insights from the large amounts of data that companies are routinely collecting, storing, and using.

We will also explore the roles that social media and internet marketing are playing in the growth of business intelligence, and how companies like Facebook are helping other companies act on data in powerful ways.

Previous technical revolutions were revolutions of *things*, and so they were easy to notice – and that revolution is still going on. Now it is being joined by a new revolution driven by data together with artificial intelligence and machine learning. While we are all touched by it, it's often not something we can see or touch! In that way, it is proceeding right under our noses, with many people barely aware of the massive and rapid changes taking place.

In this book, I hope to introduce you to these radical changes and get you excited about them. Business is in the process of being revolutionized in ways that it hasn't been since the industrial revolution.

Chapter 1: An Introduction to BI, Big Data, AI, and More

In the 17th and 18th centuries, a merger of science, technology, and capitalism gave birth to the industrial revolution. Up to that time, societies had been static. Even during the times of the great ancient civilizations in Rome, Greece, Egypt, India, and China, societies made some strides but continued their existence in relatively static form. Poverty rates remained the same from the fall of the Roman empire until the start of the industrial revolution.

As soon as the first machines were invented, society began to take off in remarkable ways. Production of goods increased as mechanical devices enhanced the capabilities of workers to manufacture everything from textiles to pins. The efficiency of factories exploded overnight, so much so that by the middle of the 19th century, the world had been completely transformed. Even by then, people were already leading radically different lives than their grandparents had done, and the revolution was only getting started.

In this chapter, after a quick review, we will briefly introduce many of the main topics discussed in this book.

Enter the Information Revolution

This revolution, as you well know, continued into the 20th century. The industrial part of the revolution continued growing, with the invention of the airplane, the automobile, the radio, television, and the distribution of electrical power into every home (at least in developed countries). But in the second world war, one of the most significant inventions of all time was quietly developed and used for some specialized tasks, such as breaking Nazi codes. This was an electronic computer. The genius engineer, Alan Turing, quickly recognized that the computer was an entirely different kind of machine. Its functions were sufficiently general that it could - at least, in theory - be imagined to work on any task. It was also something that processed information. All other machines developed to that point processed other things.

Turing recognized that a computer could mimic human intelligence. Whether or not it would be "real" intelligence was beside the point. This was a very powerful new machine, and after the war ended, the invention of the computer chip (and later, the microprocessor) ensured that computers were here to stay and that they would develop very rapidly.

The development of computer power progressed, just like anything on an exponential curve does: slow at first and gradually picking up speed. In the early days, processors were much slower than they are now, but it was memory and the ability to store data that were really the weak points in computers until the 21st century. In the beginning, people were storing information on punch cards, and then feeding those into the computer. Later, this was replaced by magnetic tape, in the first transformation from physical to purely electronic form.

As the years went by, businesses were always collecting data. But in the old world before computers, the data was hard to collect. Even though some businesses were collecting some data, it was hard to do anything with it. The bottom line was that the data was impossible to bring together and synthesize, much less to interpret and gather any insights from.

This began changing when the world wide web (or internet) arrived. Likewise, computer storage capacity and the ability to retrieve and look at data began to improve. The internet only accelerated the pace of data collection. At first, people weren't even aware this was going on, and those collecting the data weren't sure what to do with it.

The World of Big Data Begins Taking Shape

But the real story was the fact that computer memory was rapidly becoming very cheap and the capacity to store information was growing exponentially. This development was joined by advances in artificial intelligence, machine learning, and pattern recognition. The public had a fuzzy awareness of this, brought to light by occasional developments such as IBM computers defeating chess champions.

But the real action was in machine learning and the processing of data. Computer scientists had been strapped for years when it came to the development of artificial intelligence, but new paths forward came to light in the 1990s and later. Machine learning came to the forefront, and people began using computers in new ways. Rather than programming computers to do specific tasks, researchers were feeding them reams of data and letting the computers learn for themselves. It was found that computers were good at detecting patterns in data that people wouldn't be able to piece together because the data was too big - and apparently too random - for the human mind to comprehend or work with. Often the patterns that the machine learning systems were able to detect in data led to actionable insights by companies. The massive amounts of data that were being collected by companies (as well as by governments and other institutions) became known as "big data". Big data is more than just the data itself; this term incorporates the analysis of the data to reveal hidden patterns, trends, and relationships that exist. Typically, big data is related to the behaviors of people. You can think of it as the new gold of the 21st century.

This is where business intelligence began to come into full focus.

What is Business Intelligence?

We associate business intelligence with computers, data, advanced statistics, and machine learning, but the reality is business intelligence has been with us ever since people have been in business. In the distant, and even more recent past, businesses had a limited capacity to collect data and take actions based on what the data was telling them.

BUSINESS INTELLIGENCE is an incredibly broad category, and yet it plays a central role in modern business. Business intelligence begins with data collection and storage. Then it incorporates any activity, tool, or process that is used to extract actionable information and make decisions based on that information. Business intelligence can be anything from running reports on data that has been collected in the organization, to examining email communications between employees to develop better ways to foster collaboration, to using machine intelligence to improve the efficiency of logistics. The development of business intelligence has been propelled forward by advances in pattern recognition, machine learning, and artificial intelligence, along with the development of a new field that integrates many of these things under one umbrella called "data science".

Some people have likened business intelligence and big data to the fourth industrial revolution – and with good reason. Big data, artificial intelligence, and machine learning are going to be shaping the future of business and of the structure of society at large in the future. Business intelligence is sometimes referred to as "BI," following the shortened naming of artificial intelligence as "AI."

Artificial Intelligence and Machine Learning

Decades ago, Turing developed a simple test to discover if one could determine whether someone hidden behind a barrier was a human being or an artificially intelligent computer. This gave birth to the idea of artificial intelligence, whereby computer systems would be built in ways that mimic the structure of the human brain, and they would learn the way a human brain does, rather than the simplistic ways that early computers did.

Developments began in fits and starts at first! In the late 1950s, an IBM engineer built a computer system that was able to learn how to play a game of checkers. His approach was completely different than the one normally used to program computers. Rather than program the computer with thousands of lines of computer code which ran by rules and told the program what to do step-by-step, he developed his checkers-playing software in a way that it would not be programmed at all. Rather, it would learn from experience. Put another way, it would learn by being exposed to data. The term MACHINE LEARNING was used to describe how the system worked.

This first attempt at machine learning was solving a simple problem, but it was remarkably successful. The more the machine played checkers, the better it got. It seemed that the adage "practice makes perfect" applied to this intelligent computer system as well.

Machine learning is a subfield, or subset, of the field of artificial intelligence. This is the development of computer systems that are capable of learning and performing tasks that normally require human brains to do. A lot of early research in artificial intelligence involved vision, as this was one of the rare parts of the brain that was easy to understand as far as structure and operation. AI has also been used for many other specialized tasks, like speech recognition.

The idea of general intelligence in the form of an "android" or human-like robot never quite got off the ground - at least not yet. For years, this made artificial intelligence the butt of many bad jokes. It became a joke that true artificial intelligence was always "30 years away".

However, remarkable strides have been made, even if we've had to redefine the expectations and roles that artificial intelligence can play in our lives, businesses, and society. Since the early years (when people imagined the HAL 9000 computer taking over the universe), AI is now viewed more realistically. It is now regarded as a tool that can help us get many specialized tasks done, often freeing up the need for human labor, in much the same way that the early machines of the industrial revolution did.

You can think of artificial intelligence as computer systems that think and learn in ways that human intelligence does. It can be specialized in tasks like speech recognition, facial recognition, language translation, and so forth.

The development of artificial intelligence has largely gone through three major phases, although they are not mutually exclusive. The first phase involved the development of neural networks. These systems mimic the actual physical functioning of the brain. As such, computer system is divided into interconnected nodes; when the system is exposed to something, it will process the data and learn.

When a person learns something, neurons form circuits. Some neurons will strengthen their connections to other neurons, while they will weaken their connections to others. While we can describe this process, it's not understood how it works and how it is that "you" are inside your brain perceiving the information that the neurons are representing and processing. Nonetheless, neural networks mimic this structure.

An AI system that is based on a neural network will have a layer of nodes that are exposed to the data being used for learning. There are nodes that are used for output of information. In between, there are hidden layers of additional nodes. The nodes can all communicate with each other, and they have connections to each other which can be strengthened or weakened - depending on how the learning process proceeds. Keep in mind that there is no computer programmer that is directing the nodes to strengthen or weaken the connections, or to talk to these nodes over here, or those over there. This all happens independently. The computer system works and learns completely on its own. After it has been trained, it can make decisions on its own, too.

The neural network phase lasted through the 1970s. Keep in mind that neural networks are still used and it's still a hot area of research. Machine learning became the central focus of AI researchers in the 1980s, and the popularity of machine learning has continued to this day. With machine learning, which is a subset of AI, large datasets are fed to the computer system, and the machine learns from the data. This can be done using supervised learning where the machine is guided to the right answer. Alternatively, this can be done in an unsupervised fashion, and the computer is exposed to the data, and it learns on its own from the data. Machine learning has gotten extremely popular because it works, and it provides many practical applications. The third phase of AI is called deep learning. Deep learning is a form of unsupervised learning that uses neural networks.

The applications of AI are specialized, but they are no less dramatic. The advantage of AI is that the systems can learn, and the more data they are exposed to, the better they get at what they do. AI can be used for data discovery, perform repetitive and high-volume tasks that people find tedious and boring, and to add intelligence to products that people use. This, in turn, can be used to collect even more data.

Data Science

As machine learning began to enter the scene as a practical tool used by business, a new field of study emerged. This is an interdisciplinary field that combines statistics, computer science, business knowledge: data science. The job of the data scientist is to manage the use of machine learning in a business environment. The data scientist will determine what problems and dataset the machine will work with, and what questions need to be asked of the data. The data scientist will train machine learning systems and then decide when they are ready to be deployed in the real world. It is a booming field that is at the core of many trends in business today.

Data Mining

Data mining, or knowledge discovery databases (KDD), is a process of finding information that is contained in large databases. Data is raw, and by itself doesn't represent information. Data mining is a process that will determine what - if any - information is contained in the datasets.

IoT

IoT is shorthand for "internet of things". This is a long-promised merger of the internet with many common devices and appliances that we use. But in today's world, it is taking on new meaning, as it is going well beyond a simple internet connection. Now we are talking about ordinary devices being used to collect massive amounts of data about people in their home, or on their bodies in the form of wearable computers. There are many ways that these devices and data can be used and, of course, there is the ethical question of abuse and potential for hacking.

Data Analytics

Data analytics is a process of discovering useful information in datasets. It involves many levels of data processing, such as examining the data, modeling the data, and transforming it into a more useful form. The goal of data analytics is to bring data into a form that can be used to improve awareness among important actors and use it to support informed decisions that are actionable.

Cybersecurity

Cybersecurity is the protection of computers and computer systems from malicious activity that can include hacking, remote control, intentional damage, and unauthorized access. Big data and data analytics are often used to enhance cybersecurity by using machine learning and AI systems to detect irregularities that can be associated with intrusions and attacks of computer systems.

Social Media

Social media refers to a wide range of websites and apps that allow people to come together and communicate and share information.

Common examples of social media include Facebook, Twitter, Snapchat, Instagram, and Pinterest. Social media represents an unprecedented opportunity to collect data on people, their associations, and their behaviors. Although search engines and shopping sites like Amazon are not social media, the combination of data from social media sites with other computer and internet-based systems is proving to be a very powerful force.

Internet Marketing

Internet marketing is the process of advertising on the internet through search engine advertising, tailored ads on websites that are frequently visited, or through direct advertising to people on social media. Internet marketing uses big data, data analytics, machine learning, and artificial intelligence in order to tailor advertising to each individual. Internet marketing can use big data quickly, rapidly changing its approach in almost real-time based on recent behaviors of the consumer. If you visit a website for shoes and then start seeing ads for shoes on the Wall Street Journal, Facebook, and CNN, then you have experienced this practice.

Chapter 2 : An Overview of Business Intelligence

Business intelligence is being driven by artificial intelligence, machine learning, pattern recognition, data analytics, and more. But what does business intelligence (or BI, as it is commonly known) mean to businesses themselves? For the business, the real meaning of BI is going to be the result. At the core, BI is about actionable insights from the myriads of big data that exist in the company. The data can come from many sources, and oftentimes BI is about data that is collected about the company itself! This can include information about company operations, interactions between employees, meetings, communications, phone calls, emails, and so forth. Any and all information that is collected by a business is useful for BI. Internal information can be used to massively improve company efficiency and operations, while information collected about customers can be used to improve customer service, develop new products and services, and respond in real-time to customer concerns.

The Key Characteristics of BI for business

Let's begin by taking a closer look at how business intelligence can benefit a business. At the core, business intelligence is driven by data. It is also driven by the fact that modern companies need to make data-driven decisions rapidly. The goal of business intelligence is to process that data and get insights from it. This can be done with machine learning, but the goal is to provide actionable insights to the employees of the business. These insights need to be more than actionable; they need to be timely, in the sense that decisions need to be made as rapidly as possible. In today's competitive world, the competitors of any business are using these same tools to their own advantage. Those that act first – if they are acting on accurate information - are the ones that are going to come out on top. Information also *must have value.* Any old information won't do, and information that isn't valuable and accurate can lead a company astray.

Data and the information that is extracted or inferred from the data forms the core of BI. The first essential characteristic that is important for BI: the data must be genuine. Falsified or misleading data would destroy the entire enterprise. It is important for the company to ensure that it has good data sources, that the company is not being misled on purpose by other companies or bad employees within the company, and that the company's computer systems are not being attacked from the outside.

Going forward, we will assume that the data is genuine. The second key characteristic that BI must have: it must be able to provide companies with meaningful insights that have value. In order to have value, insights that are extracted from data must be able to drive important decision making. This is where the data science comes in; it's crucial to start off asking the right questions and making sure that data analytics, machine learning, and artificially intelligent systems are working on the right data that is going to be useful for actionable insights. The patterns, trends, and relationships that are discovered using machine learning need to have a significant impact on business operations. There are many ways that they can be useful:

- By cutting fuel costs

- Speeding communications between different departments and teams
- Improving collaboration
- Accelerating the delivery of products and services to customers
- Quickly identifying problems and providing solutions
- Improving customer service

Those are some of the many examples of valuable insights provided by BI. If valuable insights are not extracted from the data, then time and money are wasted, while competitors are racing ahead.

This brings us to the next key characteristic: insights gleaned from data analysis must be valuable AND ACCURATE. If the information that comes from the process of business intelligence is not accurate, then you can't say it is useful. Of course, accuracy in this context is not always absolute; there can be a range of accuracy. It might be accurate at a level of 50%, or it might be accurate at a level of 90%. If it has low accuracy, then it's not going to be valuable for the decision-making process in the organization. Insights that have low levels of accuracy are going to lead business operations in the wrong direction, wasting time, decreasing efficiency, and ultimately costing money. It could lead a company to develop the wrong kinds of products or to misallocate resources in the enterprise. When these problems come to light, trust in the process will be reduced, causing further problems.

The final key characteristic is that business intelligence needs to be rapid. Remember the old saying: "Time is of the essence." The faster you get information, the more valuable it becomes. In other words, the more important that something is, the timelier it needs to be. Still, it's important to avoid sacrificing accuracy or value for the sake of getting insights out to the organization quickly. Therefore, none of the characteristics described here can be taken to exist independently. They are all interacting and crucially important, and one depends on the other and vice versa.

While we don't want to cut corners in order to achieve the most rapid delivery of actionable information possible, one cannot underestimate the cost to a business when it comes to time delays. There are many bottlenecks in an organization, and any single one of them can severely constrict workflow.

The Four-Step Process of Business Intelligence

The core of business intelligence is actionable information. But how does this information get out to the organization, and how can it be made better? The way to make it better is to feed new data back into the system. This works particularly well when we are dealing with machine learning-based computer systems. Remember the checkers program (the game) that launched machine learning in the first place? The more the computer played the game, the better it got. This is true of machine learning systems that are used in business today.

The first step of the process is data collection. A key part of this process is ensuring that we are gathering the right data for the types of insights that we are interested in. Of course, beforehand we don't know what the insights are going to be, but we know what kinds of questions we would like to ask. It is going to be up to the machine learning systems to find out what the insights are, but they must be pointed in the right direction. And if the data is bad to begin with, the entire process becomes flawed.

Once the insights have been generated, the next step in the process is making data-driven decisions based on those insights. This can be anything depending on what the company is using the data for. For example, ad expenditures on social media sites could be increased. Perhaps a sales team will have its budget reduced. There are endless possibilities.

No matter what kinds of decisions are made, you must be prepared ahead of time to figure out how you are going to measure results. This is the third step of the process. The bottom line is you must know *what you are going to measure* in order to analyze results and draw conclusions from the process.

Finally, the operational results that come from the implementation of the actionable insights can be fed back into the system. The new data can be used to enhance learning and improve efficiency in a step-by-step fashion.

Business Intelligence Applications

There are many software tools that are used as part of the business intelligence process. These include some that are very familiar and mature, along with some new tools that have entered the corporate world in recent years. Let's look at some of these tools.

Reporting and Database Querying

Businesses have lots of data in databases, and it's important to be able to get that data out and present it in a useful fashion. SQL, or structured query language, is a key part of that process. This allows you to get data out of large databases, search it, and organize it in useful ways. You also need a way to present data in a readable format to human beings. Reporting software that works with company databases serves this purpose.

Spreadsheets

Data can be drawn together or filtered and presented in spreadsheets. Ever since their introduction in the early to mid-1980s, electronic spreadsheets have played a fundamental role in gathering data and turning it into a useful form. In case you mistakenly think that modern systems are making spreadsheets less relevant, *this is not the case!*

Data Dashboards

Dashboards are viewed on a web page. A dashboard is a computerized interface that provides the users with real-time reports that are updated in real-time using a database. The application of dashboards is widespread and can be used in any business application in which seeing real-time updates of data is useful, such as viewing inventory, staffing, or manufacturing data.

OLAP

OLAP stands for "online analytical processing". OLAP is a set of tools that helps users analyze multidimensional data. OLAP is used for business reporting, budgeting, and forecasting.

Data Mining

Data mining is a process by which large datasets are analyzed in order to detect patterns that exist in the data. It uses methods from machine learning, statistics, and from databases when large amounts of company data are stored in relational databases. The main goal of data mining is to extract data and transform it so that it can be presented in a useful and readable form. Data mining also seeks to reveal patterns that are in the data and extract useful knowledge.

Data Warehouse

A data warehouse is a computer system that serves to perform data analysis and reporting that is useful to the enterprise. A data warehouse also centralizes data collected from many different sources.

Data Cleansing

Data cleansing is a supportive but very important task in terms of maintaining the data that is used as a part of the business intelligence process. It involves the detection, repair, or deletion of corrupt database records. Data cleansing is necessary in order to continually ensure that the data used by a company is accurate.

Business Activity Monitoring

Business activity monitoring is a software system that uses data dashboards to present important information on the activities, operations, and processes taking place in an organization. The goal of business activity monitoring is to help an organization make more informed decisions that are data driven. It can help companies quickly identify problems within the organization and reallocate resources as necessary.

Real-Time BI

As computer systems continue to develop and incorporate the use of mobile technologies, the potential for using real-time data in business operations is becoming more important. Real-time data can be presented to key personnel involving business operations, inventories, advertising and marketing spending, social media contacts, email, and messaging. Data can be collected in real-time to quickly launch marketing campaigns or adjust existing advertising efforts, or to contact customers directly via email, text message, or on Facebook with tailor- crafted offers.

The Core Benefits of Business Intelligence

Business intelligence is a set of tools that can help managers and business leaders act on what the data is telling them. This can help the business respond in a timely fashion, rapidly responding to changing market conditions and fixing internal problems to improve efficiency and gain a competitive edge rapidly. Data-driven decisions allow business leaders to take a proactive stance allowing the company to become nimbler and more responsive. BI will allow the company to gain unexpected insights into their data and take the company in new and powerful directions that they would not have done otherwise. The business environment is fast-paced and dynamic, and business intelligence is going to help companies navigate this environment as it becomes even more complex, and the pace quickens. With solid data, business intelligence will also help companies make fact-based decisions, whereas in the past, they were operating in the dark. Those companies that don't utilize the tools of business intelligence are going to find themselves falling behind.

Past or Future Data?

One of the issues that are important to understand about business intelligence is that it relies on using PAST data. As such, it is interested in analyzing historical data and presenting it in an easily digestible form to members of the company. Then company members can make actionable decisions based on the data and its analysis. This can be in the form of readable reports and visualizations. Visualizations can include graphics, charts, and so forth that are readily understood by human readers.

Many other types of analysis associated with big data - in particular, machine learning and data analytics - are used for the purposes of *predictive modeling.* That is, think of business intelligence as backward-looking, gleaning insights that can be used by humans to make business decisions. Other types of data analysis are going are used to take future action or predict what different courses of action will produce. We will discuss these issues as we go forward, but one might consider that as more tools become available that utilize the ability to act in future situations and predict the what the results are going to be based on new input data, it is highly probable that business intelligence is going to evolve to incorporate these tools. You are probably going to witness business intelligence incorporating machine learning in order to develop self-service BI.

Chapter 3: BI and AI

Data and insights *from data* are at the core of business intelligence. This is where artificial intelligence and machine learning come into play. AI and machine learning help extract meaning from the data that is so crucial for business intelligence. In fact, without machine learning and artificial intelligence, business intelligence would be years behind where it is today. In this chapter, we are going to discuss the role that artificial intelligence can play in the growth and enhancement of business intelligence. Some readers may find the terms "machine learning" and "artificial intelligence" confusing. Here's a distinction: machine learning is a subset of AI and has specific uses that we will discuss in this chapter.

The core uses of AI

Artificial intelligence is going to be used in a wide variety of ways. You already see early applications of artificial intelligence in the form of self-driving vehicles, AI systems that can analyze MRI scans for signs of tumors. Language translation services are becoming nearly as accurate as a human translator. AI is used in speech recognition systems, facial recognition systems, and more. AI is at the beginning stages of development, and so the applications are only going to increase. In this section, we are going to look at the core ways that artificial intelligence is used and how it can be applied in business.

One of the ways that AI can be used is to add intelligence to existing systems. That is, AI will be added to existing products in order to transform them from dumb inanimate objects into more useful intelligent systems that can better serve the needs of their users. One area where this is already being done is adding intelligence to automobiles, such as the case of regular vehicles that are not self-driving cars. Adding limited intelligence capabilities can help drivers operate the car more safely and improve the odds of avoiding accidents.

Soon, AI can be added to a wide array of devices to connect them to the internet, collect data, and then provide upgraded capabilities as a result of making currently mundane devices useful and intelligent. For example, a toilet can use AI in order to detect early signs of disease and communicate this information to the doctor. AI can also be used to add conversational capabilities to products, better serving the needs of customers. For example, an intelligent refrigerator could let the owner know that supplies of various foods are running low, and the device could even order the food items via an internet connection. Smart machines can also be used for security or monitoring public spaces for safety.

Data processing is another area where AI can be used, and it is already being used extensively via machine learning. This is typically used to spot patterns in large datasets; that information can then be used in many different contexts by businesses. Insights from this kind of analysis have been used to improve the efficiency of logistics, cut fuel costs, improve the allocation of staff and other resources, fraud detection, and approve customers for loans and credit, among other applications. The use of machine learning is sure to grow in the coming years and become more widespread in the business community. The important thing about machine learning is that it can extract insights from large datasets that could not have been extracted in any other way.

Machine learning can also be used on internal data collected by the company. Often this kind of data is unstructured and in the form of images, recorded phone calls, and emails. Artificially intelligent systems can analyze this data for unexpected patterns that often produce actionable insights that help the company organize itself better and more efficiently.

Neural networks using deep learning are being used to detect unexpected or anomalous patterns, improving fraud detection, and cybersecurity. The increased levels of data combined with better neural networks are making these processes more useful and efficient. Like the original checkers-playing software, these systems are constantly learning and improving their skills as they are presented with more data.

AI Can Make Decisions on Its Own

Business intelligence is about gathering, processing data, and getting actionable insights from the data so that it can be presented to humans, allowing them to make decisions based on the data. Artificial intelligence adds an interesting wrinkle to this model, because AI systems - once properly trained - can make decisions independently from human supervision. AI systems are already being deployed in many contexts to perform work and make decisions that humans used to make. For example, they are used to generate credit scores and analyze loan applications, or they are used as chatbots to provide the first level of customer support. These systems work autonomously without human intervention.

The first question that comes up in this context is: How is AI going to impact BI? Let's think about it. One benefit of AI applications is that this frees up humans for more interesting work. AI is taking over the tedious types of tasks – many of which humans couldn't perform anyway. Think of big data in this context. A human mind is not even capable of examining big data and extracting insights from it. So, in a sense, a new job has been created for AI to perform that didn't even exist without AI. In a lot of cases, AI can help an organization become more efficient by removing the need for people to be involved in many tasks that rely on tedious data analysis, moving humans into roles that are more valuable because they require insight and they are far less tedious. Think about how AI is automatically enhancing the security of the organization by being able to search out anomalous behaviors on computer networks in order to provide better cybersecurity.

According to the Harvard Business Review, the use of AI in business falls into three general categories. Let's look closely at each of these.

Process Automation

Process automation is becoming a very common application in businesses increasingly driven by AI. Process automation involves using intelligent computer systems to perform administrative tasks in a business. These can include (as we noted above) handling frontline communications with customers, updating databases, sending out bills, and recording documentation.

Cognitive Insights

This is a more advanced use of AI in business. These are machine learning systems that become better at their jobs as time passes because they can learn from data that they encounter continually. These types of systems are used for pattern recognition, development of tailored advertising, cybersecurity, and to predict customer behavior.

Cognitive Engagement

These types of systems are designed to interact directly with the public, and with employees. They can include intelligent phone systems that offer customer support or take bill payments, chatbots, customer service, or systems that give medical advice. AI systems can also be used to develop personal health coaches, reminding people to take their medications, examine dietary choices, and making sure people have kept up with their exercise plans.

How AI will Take BI to a new level

The purpose of business intelligence is to extract meaning and insight from a company's data. Artificial intelligence is going to enhance this process massively. AI is not going to replace all people, but it will help to process the large amounts of data that companies are collecting and turn it into useful information. AI will also play a role in analyzing that information and synthesizing it to help humans make better decisions based on the data. AI will also be able to play a role in assessing the integrity and value of the data. The higher speeds at which AI and machine learning systems can operate allows them to analyze company data much faster and better than any human. This can mean that AI systems can synthesize data and do preliminary processing, saving people from having to do a lot of tedious work.

Another area where AI is going to be used more and more is in the area of improving business intelligence with the use of *predicting modeling*. This can be incorporated into business intelligence to predict the outcomes of different courses of action before implementing them. Then, using the results from such modeling, the best solution that is identified can be the one that is put into practice.

Chapter 4: BI and Big Data

In the modern era, big data is playing an ever-increasing role. Corporations have collected massive datasets about their customers and about their own internal operations. With machine learning, businesses can extract valuable information about the data that would otherwise be impossible. As explained earlier: human beings lack the capacity to analyze large datasets and find relationships in them. But for artificially intelligent machines, this is an easy task. Not all patterns, trends, and relationships found in the data are going to be useful for the company - or even cost-effective. The role of business intelligence when it comes to big data is to determine whether it's actionable, accurate, and valuable information.

Big Data Classifications

There are three general classifications of big data: unstructured, structured, and semi-structured. All three types of data can be mined for information that might be of use.

Structured Data

Structured data is *organized data*. It is stored in relational databases and other organized data structures, and it's based on a data model that can represent something like a product in inventory or a customer. The data model will flesh out the properties that the company wants to track. An example of structured data would be an employee listing in a database that had the employee's name, age, salary, home address, and so on. The elements, or records, in a relational database have addresses that can be used to look up individual records easily. Structured data can typically be queried using structured query language or SQL so that subsets of the data can be extracted from the database. The data can be sorted, grouped, or filtered as desired. Structured data has been with businesses and used in business intelligence for several decades now. SQL was developed by IBM in the early 1970s, and over the following decades the use of relational databases became more common, growing in sophistication and usability. As soon as data was organized into databases like Microsoft Access, programs were built to utilize it. Information from databases is easy to analyze and present in the form of reports or on data dashboards.

Each element in a record in a structured dataset is called a field. Fields can be one of several basic data types such as alphanumeric or text, numeric, or currency. An employee's name or their social security number would be a field. Data can be queried from multiple databases and combined into single records using a runtime command, providing new information that could be useful to the business. For example, a business could have a database of customers and a separate database of past purchases by a customer. These could be combined to yield useful information about each customer or about products. For example, if the company had each customer's address, it could pull up reports that showed how each product sold in different locations.

Spreadsheets represent another form of structured data that has also been a critical component of business intelligence. A spreadsheet has the advantage of providing a unified platform that can contain the data, together with an analysis of the data and graphical presentation. Analysis can be changed in real-time to get new insights from the data. Spreadsheets arose from older methods of working with data on paper, but soon revealed the exponential increase in power that they offered when looking at data and gathering insights from it. As soon as computerized spreadsheets became available, companies flocked to them in large numbers. The first commercially available spreadsheet programs were made in the early 1980s; by the end of the decade, nearly every business was using them.

Structured data has many characteristics that have made it easy for humans to work with, including easy data entry and the ability of computers to quickly pull up data and organize it into useful forms such as graphics, pie charts, histograms, or reports.

Even though structured data is highly organized and easily interpreted by humans, there can be insights into the data that humans are not able to extract. The reason is that the datasets have grown incomprehensibly large, and there are large numbers of ways that related databases can be combined. Once combined, each new combination of data yields an exponentially number of useful insights for the business. This is where machine learning has come into play. Before the past decade, the processing of structured data was done with "dumb" computers that processed data without thinking about it. These were conventional computer systems that only implemented the instructions that were given to them by computer programmers, and they followed a pre-determined set of rules. Those types of computer systems are good for mundane tasks, but they are not able to think, interpret, or act autonomously in the way that artificially intelligent systems can.

Unstructured Data

Big data can also be unstructured. This is information that is not stored in a relational database or some other data structure-based form such as a spreadsheet. You can consider this type of data as the opposite of structured data. It is not easily addressable by SQL or pulled together and analyzed by humans.

Today, most data collected by businesses is unstructured data. It is estimated that about 90% of the data collected is unstructured, and this percentage is likely to increase in the coming years. This is going to make machine learning more important for the business since it plays a central role in analyzing unstructured data.

The business has many forms of unstructured data. This can include multimedia content such as images, videos, and even slide show presentations. Although you may think of text as structured data many text-based documents are unstructured data. This can include social media messages, text messages sent over mobile networks, emails, memos, and word processing documents. Images, like a word processing document, are highly organized in and of themselves. However, a collection of millions of images or word processing documents that a business may have stored is completely unstructured. So unstructured data has internal structure, but the collection of data is unstructured. The collection of data would be difficult if not impossible to organize into a database or spreadsheet, and even if it could be organized in such fashion, it would be extremely difficult and time consuming to extract information from it. The internal structure in unstructured data such as emails or images can contain extremely useful information.

You can imagine the problems that would arise while using humans to try to organize and analyze unstructured data. A program like Microsoft Excel would not be capable of analyzing images and organizing them as a result, much less finding actionable information from the images. A human being might be able to do it, for example, by examining each image submitted by a user on a social media site, classifying the image in some way. However, to go through large datasets, a human being would take thousands of years or more just to get through it. Mistakes would be made, and insights would be missed. Human beings would also suffer from fatigue, slowing any analysis of such data and causing even more mistakes.

Gaining insights from the data and relating different data from the same person (for example, images uploaded, and text messages sent) makes this task utterly impossible for human analysis and even traditional analysis used with structured data.

Until the development of machine learning, effectively working with unstructured data was impossible. Machine learning allows data to be mined, processed, and analyzed to find hidden patterns that can be used to create actionable insights for business.

This is an important development for businesses because large data stores of unstructured data contain a lot of information which can lead to better and more informed business decisions. Since the internet became widespread in the late 1990s and computer storage capacity increased, the collection of unstructured data by companies of all sizes has grown exponentially, and it continues to expand with each passing year. In fact, the pace of collection of unstructured data is quickening, making the ability to process it and analyze it very important for business intelligence.

Just searching through the data is a challenge in and of itself. Software tools have been developed that help companies mine and organize the data. It can then be presented to machine learning systems that can glean actionable insights from the data.

Unstructured data can come from multiple sources. When people think of unstructured data, an example that comes to mind is social media. Each individual or business using social media is creating a large set of unstructured data that includes images, videos, tweets, postings, comments, or messages sent to other users.

However, there is also a large amount of unstructured data that is being collected internally by businesses on their employees. This includes emails, memos, word processing documents, video footage of facilities, and even logs of computer usage. This information - if it could be analyzed - would provide an endless array of actionable insights for business intelligence that could be used to improve the efficiency of the company.

These benefits can work across a large spectrum of applications. For example, one use of logging computer time is to identify employees who are unproductive or who waste time at work by logging into Facebook or spending too much time reading personal emails or checking favorite websites. This allows the company to weed out unproductive employees - or at least give them a chance to adjust their behavior.

Tracking of employees is now possible, so companies can know where employees are at all times and how they are spending their time inside company facilities. However, it's not enough to just have the tracking data. The quantity of the data can explode very quickly. To become useful, the data must be gathered, analyzed, and then interpreted so that it can be used with business intelligence to improve operations.

The list of possible unstructured data sources is endless, as are the possibilities of gleaning actionable information. For example, emails between employees can contain a treasure trove of information. By analyzing emails, a company could find better ways to organize staff and encourage collaboration to improve efficiency. It can also be used to spot waste, fraud, and abuse that could be occurring inside the organization.

The key to using unstructured data and getting actionable insights from it is machine learning.

Semi-Structured Data

The third class of data exists that is in between structured and unstructured data. This is data that is a mixture of structured and unstructured data, or at least it contains data that could be organized as structured data.

The Five V's of Big Data

When people talk about "Big Data," they often talk about the five V's. In fact, in recent years some have expanded this to the six V's. These are characteristics that describe big data. These include:

- Volume: Big data is a lot of data. It can be collected from multiple sources.

- Velocity: Big data is being generated at an increasingly rapid pace.
- Variability: Big data comes in a wide variety of forms, and the ways that big data can be used are infinite.
- Variety: This refers to the types of big data described in the last section – structured, unstructured, and semi-structured data.
- Veracity: How reliable is the data? This is a measure of how much the data can be trusted.
- Value: The final "V" on our list is the key one for business intelligence. This is the value of big data, and whether it is actionable for the business.

Keep in mind that not all data has value. In fact, whether data can provide actionable insights doesn't just depend on how revolutionary the discoveries made from the data are. There are going to be many practical considerations. For example, an amazing insight discovered by AI about data a company has would not have value if implementing any actions based on it are not cost-effective. Another possibility is that it may be impractical for the company to carry out.

Nonetheless, it's clear that companies that are analyzing their big data are going to be the companies that gain a competitive advantage. Although some insights won't be actionable from a practical standpoint, many will be. This will lead to better relationships with customers. It will help the company allocate resources better. Companies using big data will be able to develop better products and services, and they will be able to respond to maintenance and support issues with targeted efficiency. In addition, they will be able to restructure their organizations in real-time in order to massively improve efficiency, collaboration, and throughput. In short, they will gain massive competitive advantages – and we see that big data plays a central role in business intelligence.

How do Big Data and Business Intelligence Compare?

This is a question that often comes to mind among people learning about these topics. However, the question comes from confusion about what big data and business intelligence are. Business intelligence is the complete set of data, tools, insights, and actions that arise from the data that a business has access to. Business intelligence leads to data-driven decision making.

Big data is nothing more than data, and it's not useful unless it can be searched, organized, and analyzed. So, you cannot compare big data to business intelligence.

Big data is a component of modern business intelligence. If you recall from our earlier discussions of business intelligence, it begins with the data; this is where you will find the connection between big data and business intelligence. It is a part of the foundation upon which business intelligence is built. In fact, today, you can say that for many companies, big data IS the foundational component of business intelligence.

Big Data Resources

Big data can be an expansive resource for companies. This is because many sources of big data exist, and they are accessible to businesses as big data becomes the new currency. Therefore, a company is not limited to the data that it collects on its own. Big data is a large component of buying and selling between businesses these days and has been for decades. In past years, businesses could buy customer lists from other businesses. Today, you can buy big data and even have it analyzed for you, as we will show with our case study for small business below. The key point here is that businesses should not be limited in their thinking process about data. They should recognize that data sources exist for them inside and outside the company.

Developing a big data strategy

A big data strategy is going to involve the collection, storage, retrieval, analysis, and actionable insights. The goal of a big data strategy is to build a big data foundation that can power business intelligence.

The collection is not an issue for most businesses, but many businesses err by pre-judging the value of data that they could collect, thus not collecting as much data as they should. By now, you should recognize that data may have insights that are not readily apparent. This is the benefit of machine learning and the role that it plays in data analysis: finding hidden patterns that humans didn't know existed and - frankly – couldn't have known existed. Therefore, you need to collect data with an open mind. Any bit of information that a business can collect is potentially useful. At first glance, it might appear of no consequence, but it might be used later to draw unexpected connections that can lead to data-driven decisions later.

The second issue that needing addressed as part of a big data strategy is the *storage and retrieval of the data*. A large amount of infrastructure is needed to handle the volume and velocity of big data. This includes large storage capacity as well as powerful computers. It is difficult for organizations - especially smaller to mid-sized businesses - to build the kind of data-driven infrastructure that will enable them to handle big data effectively. Doing so could literally require hundreds of computer servers with huge banks of data storage and highly efficient data retrieval tools. In addition, a high level of cybersecurity is necessary to protect the integrity of the data.

For many businesses, these requirements mean that they are going outside the organization to have these needs met. Cloud computing has made this possible, and many of the world's largest companies are offering accessible cloud computing resources that are cost-effective, fast, and easily used to store and retrieve data on a 24/7 basis. Providers of such services include Amazon, Microsoft, and Google. These companies offer several levels of cloud services that can be tailored to fit the needs of any business size, from a one-person operation running as a home business up to a large corporation - or even government entity. For example, Amazon's Simple Storage Service, known as Amazon S3, can be used by businesses of any size for low-cost cloud computing services.

Companies that can deploy their own big data systems can utilize open source tools to get the job done. This includes using Apache tools such as Hadoop and Spark, along with MapReduce. Careful considerations must be made. Handling the job internally will keep the data under the direct control of the company. However, this will entail having to build out or rent massive computer storage capacity that must be maintained on a 24/7 basis. That will also require a robust set of information security measures to ensure the integrity of the data and protect it from hacking, corruption, and other problems. This will also require hiring a large amount of staffing.

Even though many larger businesses might have the capacity to implement their own completely internal big data strategy, it's not clear that doing so is always the best way forward. This decision will have to be made by each organization. However, the fact that established companies like Microsoft and IBM are available for providing infrastructure and services that are already thoroughly tested and robust makes outsourcing these tasks a viable and more cost-effective option.

By utilizing third-party services, you can massively reduce the cost of implementing a big data strategy. Big data capabilities will be provided for you by established companies that have already developed massive computer infrastructure for storing, maintaining, and securing data. Third-party sources like IBM, Google, and Microsoft may also be able to assist with analytics.

Once the collection, storage, and retrieval problems are solved, systems must be put in place to make sense of the data. By itself, the data is useless. To be used for the kind of data-driven decision making that business intelligence entails, the patterns, relationships, and trends in the data must be discovered and put in a presentable form for human analysis. These steps will involve the use of data science and machine learning. This is another step where a company will have to decide whether it wants to do this internally or outsource the task.

There are several arguments that can be made for outsourcing the task for small and mid-sized businesses. Many companies like IBM have a long history of developing artificial intelligence and machine learning tools, and they are making their capabilities available as business services they are providing for clients at an effective cost. IBM has been a leader in this area since artificial intelligence first became a field, so you know you are getting high levels of reliability. This is not a recommendation for or against IBM, but rather to let you know that these types of services are available. They are also available from other large companies like Microsoft, Facebook, and Google, as well as from many newer and startup companies.

Many large corporations are doing this internally. Southwest Airlines is one example.

Either way, a part of your big data strategy is going to include developing a data science team. If you outsource your big data analysis, you may still need an internal data scientist to collaborate with third-party teams to get the most out of the data. Data scientists can be hired internally, or you can work with contract providers.

Machine learning tools for doing data analysis is also available for internal use, and you can hire data scientists to develop their own tools. Depending on your specific needs, there may be off-the-shelf software tools that you can use, and they are already proven to be reliable and effective. For this reason, you may not necessarily want to hire a team of data scientists to develop your own internal tools. Of course, if the expense can be managed and there are special needs in a company that cannot be addressed by off-the-shelf components, this can be an option to pursue as a part of your big data strategy. Another alternative is to utilize existing services from companies like IBM, Google, and Microsoft to turn your big data into insights that can be incorporated into business intelligence.

The final part of a big data strategy is engaging in data-driven decision making based on the actionable insights that have been derived from this process. This is going to become a central part of the business process, operation, and organization. This is because it is a continuous process. Machine learning is not a one-time event; it is going on constantly as large volumes of data continue to be collected. It operates in this way to be able to provide new insights often on a real-time basis after the infrastructure has been established.

In each case, the actionable insights provided by this process are going to provide a basis for business intelligence as well as provide inputs for business intelligence. Human insight and ingenuity will be brought to bear in many cases. Not every insight is going to have an equal value to the enterprise. Therefore, all the existing components of business intelligence will have to be applied in order to determine which actions can and should be taken by the organization. Issues such as cost-effectiveness are going to be central, as well as the ability of the company to carry out each action from a practical standpoint. The allocation of limited resources to different possible actions is another factor. The leaders of the business at all levels of management will have to weigh each possible action against others. This is nothing new, and businesses may have to forgo some actionable insights even if they are valuable in favor of others that are going to be impactful and be more cost-effective. The situation will have to be evaluated and re-evaluated on a consistent basis as more data continues to come in.

Not all possible actions that come out of the application of machine learning and AI to big data are going to require the input of humans. In many cases, these systems will be operating autonomously and without human input, other than a periodic review. Examples of these types of applications include cybersecurity and fraud detection in financial matters.

Many people new to the concept of machine learning are hesitant – even put off - by the autonomous capabilities that it offers. However, this can be a huge competitive advantage to the organization. Rather than making humans useless, it frees them up so they can be used for higher-level and more important tasks. It also helps the company work far more efficiently, both internally and externally. An example of this is frontline customer support operations. By using an AI system to handle this, employees can be dedicated to handle customer problems that are of a more serious and impactful nature. This will improve the ability of the company to respond to customer complaints and problems by providing better service. However, one side-effect of this: companies and society at large will have to devote more resources to employee training so that they are able to perform at a higher level that requires a larger and more sophisticated job skillset.

Problems with Big Data

The value of actionable insights arising from big data is only as good as the original datasets themselves. As they say in computer science: "Garbage in, garbage out" (GIGO). Errors in big data can occur at the collection point of the data, but data can also be misinterpreted. But, for businesses to have the most efficient and beneficial big data strategy that they can possibly have, they need to begin at the point of data collection.

In many cases, there is not enough data collected, as paradoxical as that sounds. While companies may have large amounts of data, they may also be trying to get insights from DATA POINTS that are not known in enough detail in order to bring actionable insights.

Analysis of big data also suffers from a problem referred to as the *bias-variance problem*. This is closely related to machine learning, and we will discuss this problem in a later chapter. But be aware that the bias-variance problem - if not handled correctly by data science professionals - can lead to erroneous conclusions.

Another problem that can plague big data is that large errors can occur when fictitious statistical relationships are derived from the data. Since people have great faith in the infallibility of computers, they often ignore the fact that bad data could have been inputted to the computer system, or the data may have been presented or analyzed in the wrong way. This can lead to data-driven decisions that are based on completely or partially incorrect insights. This mistake can costly for businesses and decrease competitiveness.

Often, the data is good. But one problem with large amounts of data is that it will always include noise and outliers; both can lead to erroneous insights. When data is presented to people, they can sometimes be led astray by outliers that are not truly representative of the data. This is a problem that happens all the time.

Errors are common with the applications of big data, and machine learning systems can often misinterpret the actions of people. Consider the behavior of people online. Specially tailored advertising is all the rage among businesses these days. However, something that often occurs is that someone may look at a product or article for reasons not related at all to their own consumer behavior. For example, a friend may ask you to look something up. But the AI systems that are collecting data about you may not know about this, and they will make the mistake of believing that you are looking it up because you are interested in it. Or maybe you read about something in an article, and then look up a related product on Amazon based on nothing but curiosity from the article. You will soon be bombarded by advertisements that you have no intention of clicking on, much less acting on. In this sense, machine learning and AI systems are actually "dumb." Businesses need to familiarize themselves with weaknesses as well as the benefits of big data. Unfortunately, people are so enamored with the concepts of big data, machine learning, and artificial intelligence, that they are only willing to see the upsides while ignoring potential problems. Keep in mind that the cost of the problems can be huge if they are ignored.

Focusing only on the upsides can lead to a business having false confidence in the insights derived from big data.

One way to address many of the errors that arise from big data is to limit the sizes of datasets that are exposed to computer systems. The larger the dataset, the more likely it is that it will contain frivolous and erroneous data. Noise increases with the size of the dataset, and the larger the dataset, the more likely it is to contain outliers that are not useful for actionable information.

Another issue related to problems with big data is integrity and security. The way that big data is derived is important. A business needs to be certain that the data they are using is derived from reliable and accurate sources. Although big data seems to create the appearance of enhanced reliability – and generally it does – technology can cut multiple ways. One development that can arise from the improvements in technology is that malicious actors also have many toolsets they can use. The obvious example is hacking to expose data. However, malicious actors could also create large amounts of false data that could be used to mislead competitors. That data may be "available" to companies from external sources, or a company could have its own data compromised and corrupted, and the company may not even be aware of it. This can be costly down the road if false, misleading, or corrupted data is used to drive decision making. Machine learning and AI systems may not be capable of detecting false or misleading data. Their insights, once again, are only as good as the data that starts the process.

One result of this is that cybersecurity is going to be playing an ever more important role in business intelligence through its use in ensuring the integrity of data that companies have access to.

Another error that can occur is from the sources of data that could be fake. This is even a problem on social media sites. For example, many large Twitter accounts have fake followers. These followers can be robots that even post messages on these accounts. Many Facebook profiles are fake, and even use real people - or images from real people - to create their entirely fake profiles that can be used for malicious purposes. These issues can create problems when it comes to collecting and interpreting a large amount of unstructured data that is available through social media. The ability of social media companies to go through this data and identify false and misleading data is going to become more important as the years go by.

Small Business Case Study: Advertising Using Lookalike Audiences

Many small business owners feel overwhelmed by the concept of big data and feel like using big data, and the power of machine intelligence is beyond their reach. However, this is false, and in many cases, it's easy to leverage the data and machine learning capabilities of large corporations. One prominent example of this is lookalike audiences used for Facebook advertising.

Facebook advertising is a huge resource and game-changer for small businesses. By making its data available to any advertiser, Facebook enables small businesses to reach and target prospects in ways that were never possible before.

However, it goes beyond that. Small companies can exploit their own data, as well as data available from third-party sources by using the machine learning capabilities that Facebook has and makes available to advertisers.

Let's say that you are selling a product that would be used for horse training. You can collect a large amount of data from this. For example, you can run advertisements on Facebook, and while – at first – they may not be that effective, over time you will collect a database of users that have responded to the advertisement. You will not know much about the users, but you will have enough information that can be exploited by Facebook in order to get amazing insights.

In addition, you will probably be able to obtain data on other customers from other companies that have purchased horse training products. These can be used separately or together with the data that you have collected. Keep in mind that we are not talking about using data in the old way. In the old days, if you were able to obtain a database of people who had purchased horse training products, you could try marketing your product directly to these people. However, in the age of machine intelligence, we are going to take a different and more effective approach.

This data can be uploaded to Facebook. Then, Facebook will use its machine learning tools to analyze the data. It will discover hidden patterns, relationships, and trends that are in the data that might be completely invisible to human observers. Once it finds out these patterns, it will then use them to build a database of people for you from their general audience. These people will be connected by the hidden patterns that are present in the data whether they have purchased a horse training product or have not. This happens because they share the hidden characteristics that have been discovered through the application of machine learning; they are extremely likely to purchase horse training products.

The database that they create for you, above, is called a lookalike audience. Once it has been constructed, the small business can then run advertisement campaigns to this lookalike audience. These campaigns are far more effective than traditional advertising.

This example shows how a small business can leverage the power of third-party services to use big data together with machine learning, without having that capability themselves.

Chapter 5: BI And Machine Learning

Without machine learning, the big data that is now available to businesses, and that can be used to drive business intelligence, would be virtually useless. It is machine learning that converts reams of data into useable insights that can support data-driven decision making by human elements of the enterprise. In this chapter, we are going to take a closer look at machine learning so that you will get a better understanding of what it is, how data is used in conjunction with machine learning and the applications that machine learning has in the real world. When you understand these issues, you will be able to grasp the importance of machine learning as a focal point in business intelligence going into the future. The fact is that businesses that effectively leverage machine learning are going to have large competitive advantages in tomorrow's marketplace.

What is Machine Learning?

Machine learning involves computer systems and intelligent algorithms that can learn from the data they are exposed to. When a computer system is using machine learning, it does not need to be explicitly programmed, and it is generally not acting according to pre-defined rules telling it what to do. Moreover, machine learning systems continually learn from new data that they encounter. In this way, they act as human intelligence acts, refining themselves when learning more from every new exposure to data. This allows machine learning systems to improve their performance with time, even after being deployed in real-world applications. This type of development hasn't been seen in actively deployed computer systems before. Two examples of where this learning ability in real-time is very useful include cybersecurity and fraud detection. The more data that the systems are exposed to, the better they get at finding a fraudulent activity or increasing the security of information systems that are under their watch. It is interested and important to note that this all takes place autonomously and without human input once the systems are deployed and in use.

Classifications of Machine Learning

There are several major classifications of machine learning, but you should be aware of them without boxing in your thinking. We begin by considering regression problems. These types of problems can be handled using algorithms based on an appropriate type of regression. The parameters used in the algorithms will be discovered through the exposure of the system to data. Examples of general applications when it comes to regression problems *include predictive analysis and forecasting.* These abilities are completely general and therefore can be applied to a wide array of specific applications. For example, forecasting can be used to predict the failure of a key component in a manufacturing facility. It can also be used to predict future market decisions or to predict the behavior of customers that deal with the company. Machine intelligence, when applied to forecast, can also be used to develop more accurate weather forecasting and to make predictions for stock market behavior and to invest.

The second type of application for machine learning is called *classification.* Once again, this has a broad scope. There are many classification problems that are suitable for use with machine learning. One of the earliest applications of machine learning to classification problems was the use of machine learning in spam detection. While the system is still not perfect, it has greatly improved the robustness of email systems, allowing users to clear their email inboxes of unwanted spam emails. Spam detection is considered one of the classic examples of the classification problem.

There are many other types of classification problems that can use machine learning. These include image analysis. For example, you could use image analysis to classify images as to whether the image contains a person, a dog, or only material objects. Medical diagnostics can sometimes be framed in terms of a classification problem. By presenting X-ray or MRI images to computer systems, images can be classified based on whether they have a tumor in the image.

Another application of classification is fraud detection. By studying outlier behavior, a machine learning system can classify network access attempts as valid or invalid or look at debit card usage and automatically shut off a debit card that shows evidence of fraud. Although errors sometimes occur, the benefits far outweigh the inconvenience of occasional misidentification. And when that happens, remember that machine learning algorithms are not static. Like people, they are constantly learning, and so they learn from their mistakes, and their ability to correctly classify improves with time.

The next type of machine learning you need to be aware of is called *clustering*. Often data points can be clustered together based on certain characteristics. If you have a large and diverse population in a city, although people may be living in many different areas, you can analyze the data and regroup it, say, by education level. The data can then be used to identify shared characteristics that people with certain education levels may have, and then develop new algorithms based on these insights. Clustering can be applied to different applications with a wide range of complexity.

A similar example of clustering from a completely different application could be image analysis. Pixels are naturally distributed by location within the image, but using clustering, we can group pixels together by color instead. This ability can lead to speedier information processing, since actions on specific clusters of data can be completed faster once they have been identified. Thresholds are often used to determine how close a given object in the dataset is to a cluster, and a distance function can be used to quantify that closeness. Clustering has a wide range of applications, including product recommendations, as well as database and customer segmentation.

Next, we come to *reinforcement learning*. This type of learning involves the distribution of rewards, and this can be done with computer systems or humans using computer systems. This can be used in real-time decision making and marketing. For example, reinforcement learning can be used to send out coupons to customers at appropriate intervals. One big application of reinforcement learning is in the design of video games. By giving rewards at appropriate intervals, the video game creator can keep players in the game longer, enticing them to come back to play the game repeatedly. AI used in video game development is proving to be quite effective. Reinforcement learning can also be used on AI systems themselves, aiding them in skills acquisition.

Next, we come to *dimensionality reduction*. Often, there are too many features of any object when it comes to machine learning. The number of features that characterize an object is often referred to as *the dimension*. While large numbers of dimensions contain a large amount of information, higher numbers of dimensions also make it more difficult to arrive at that information. By using dimensionality reduction, problems can be made more practical, allowing machine learning systems to be more effective at accurately identifying hidden patterns and relationships that occur in the data.

Training Machine Learning Systems

As the name implies, a machine learning system must learn from data. There are three ways that an AI system can learn from data. These are called supervised learning, unsupervised learning, and semi-supervised learning. We now consider each in turn.

Supervised Learning

Supervised learning is used when there is already something known about past data that has been collected. In this case, there are known outputs for given inputs in the data. This type of data is well-suited for use in classification problems or with regression. For example, spam email can be classified as spam or not-spam based on characteristics of the email, and there is a large amount of past data that can be used to verify these facts.

Supervised learning, therefore, is used to map inputs to outputs. We say that the data used to train the artificially intelligent system is *labeled*. Labeled data allows us to present the system with input vectors, which are collections of features that characterize the object of study. Vectors can contain any number of dimensions, but one of the challenges for researchers and engineers is getting the number of dimensions right for each problem they encounter.

By exposing the system to input vectors with known outputs, the system can derive the relationships that exist between the input vectors and the known outputs. The goal of this kind of training is to help the machine learn enough so that it can develop the correct algorithm that describes the relationship between the input vectors and the outputs. This relationship may be completely unknown to humans, and in fact, it is probably unknown, because if people know the relationship between inputs and outputs, they can explicitly program a computer to implement that knowledge in an algorithm that can be applied to new data. So, in this situation, you are not going to know what the relationship is, but if the training is done correctly, the machine learning system will discover it.

Once the system has been trained, it will be able to correctly derive outputs for new inputs that it has never seen before. When engineers have the assurance that this process is working correctly, the system can be deployed in the real world, where it will presumably correctly identify outputs from new inputs that are coming in with new and previously unseen data. Remember that these systems continue to learn once they are deployed, so the ability of the system to do its job correctly will increase with time if the training has been done correctly to minimize total error.

Supervised learning generally goes through five steps. These are:

- Deciding on the datasets to use in training. This is a key step, and if the engineers don't get this step right, the entire process is not going to work correctly.
- Gathering data. Input data for the computer must be gathered and put in the form of input vectors, with each element of the vector being a feature of the object under study.
- Choosing the structure of the algorithm to be used. There are many choices, and based on the situational requirements, the engineers will have to use their judgment for the best algorithm. Examples include regression or decision trees.
- Training. This is the exposure of the machine learning system to the training input vectors and known outputs. The training will help the system determine the algorithmic relationship between the inputs and outputs, so that future outputs can be simply calculated for new, previously unseen inputs.
- Evaluation. The engineers will evaluate the results of the training. Training with more data can be conducted if necessary. Otherwise, the system can be deployed when an acceptable level of error is reached. To evaluate training, an unrelated set of test data can be used to determine if the system can get the correct outputs with an acceptable level of accuracy.

Issues with Supervised Learning

Supervised machine learning suffers from a problem called the *bias-variance tradeoff*. Variance is the spread - or variability - of predictions made by the system. If a system has a high level of variance, this means that it will have trouble generalizing from the training data to new datasets. In this case, it will have to overfit to the datasets it has been exposed to in training.

Bias is an error when the average output predicted by the system has a large error with respect to the correct value. Systems with high bias cannot fit the predicted outputs to the actual outputs in the training data very well.

The best approach to machine learning with systems trained using supervised learning techniques is to try to minimize the error of bias and variance *simultaneously*. You want a system with low bias and with low variance. This can be a difficult trade-off in practice.

If a system has input vectors with a dimensionality that is too small, this means that the model is too simple for the application. This will lead to high bias and low variance. The solution, in this case, is to redesign the model such that there are more features added to the input vectors.

The opposite problem can also occur. A system might have too many features in the input vector. In this case, we have a dimensionality problem. There are too many dimensions to the problem (i.e., the number of features in the input vector, which is called the dimensionality), making the detection of patterns by the machine learning system too difficult and error prone. Systems that have too many input features are going to have high variance but low bias. The way to deal with this is for the engineers to remove irrelevant or less relevant features.

Noise is another problem that can occur in large datasets. High levels of noise can cause the system to create false relationships between inputs and outputs that don't really exist. When there is a lot of noise in the input data, engineers cannot seek exact matching between inputs and outputs. In this case, they should increase bias and seek a lower variance.

Unsupervised Learning

The goal of unsupervised learning is to find previously unknown patterns in large datasets. So, in this case, the outputs are unknown for the inputs. In fact, the engineers may not even know what outputs exist for the datasets. This type of analysis is going to be used to extract previously hidden information that exists within the data.

Therefore, with unsupervised learning, pre-existing labels are not used. That is, there are no input and output labels used on the training data. It is entirely up to the machine learning system to determine what is in the data and identify it.

One type of analysis that is used with unsupervised learning is called cluster analysis. Think about the way that objects or people can be clustered or grouped together in different ways. Consider the students in high school. They are naturally clustered by class. However, they could be clustered in many ways: grouped together by height, by gender, or by height and gender. They could be clustered according to IQ or by hair color. Objects in the real world can be grouped together in an infinite number of ways, and this can be done depending on the usefulness of a given application.

When objects are clustered, the machine learning system can then extract algorithmic relationships that exist between them. This can then be used to gather insights or to act.

Unsupervised learning is also used for anomaly detection. That is, the system seeks to find outliers and determine algorithmic relationships to detect outliers when presented with new data.

We also have *neural networks*. These are structured in an analogous way to the brains of animals. Nodes represent neurons, having weighted connections to other nodes in the systems. When exposed to data, the neural networks will increase or decrease the weightings between different nodes, learning the data in the process and developing an algorithm to use on similar data in the future, based on the weighting between the nodes.

In all cases, these algorithms are not based on any explicit computer programming or definitions of rules.

Semi-Supervised Learning

It is also possible to use semi-supervised learning to train machine learning systems. In this case, the training will be divided into two distinct phases. In the first phase, the system is trained on a small subset of data using labeled inputs. That is, the first round of training is carried out using supervised learning. After this is completed, the system is then taken through another learning phase, this time using different datasets for unsupervised learning.

Some Current Applications of Machine Learning

Machine learning has been rapidly deployed in the marketplace in a wide variety of applications. In this section, we are going to briefly review some of the most common uses of machine learning to date. This might help you determine ways that machine learning could be deployed in your own business operations.

- Financial Services: Machine learning is being used on a widespread basis in financial services. This includes fraud detection, predictive investing, credit scores, and loan approvals.
- Spam Detection: This is a classic example of a classification problem that has been solved using machine learning.
- Virtual Assistants: Siri and Alexa are examples of using machine learning to help consumers search for information and complete certain tasks using vocal commands combined with machine intelligence.
- Predictive Analysis: Machine learning is routinely used to give product recommendations, predict future economic behavior and conditions, and do weather forecasting.

- Marketing and sales: Machine learning is being used for targeted advertising and improved marketing, helping companies identify the best marketing channels and approaches that will help them grow their businesses.
- Traffic prediction: Machine learning can be used to analyze traffic flows and redirect resources to keep things moving smoothly.
- Allocation of resources: By using machine learning, law enforcement agencies can predict where future crimes will occur and how this will vary with time. They can then allocate police forces in a proactive fashion before the criminal activity occurs. Resource allocation based on machine learning is also being used to allocate staffing in hospitals, and better positioning nursing and other staff to better meet patient needs.
- Video Surveillance: Humans can have trouble managing large amounts of video surveillance. Instead, machine learning systems can be deployed that can then alert human actors when anomalies are detected.
- Cybersecurity: Machine learning is being used to maintain the security of computer networks, prevent unauthorized access, and detect malware and other suspicious activities.
- Social media and access: Machine learning is being used for facial recognition, recognizing similar images, and gathering people you may know to help you establish better connections.
- Online customer support: By providing frontline customer support, machine learning systems free up human labor for other purposes and help businesses reduce overall costs.
- Self-Driving Cars: These are a good example of machine learning systems getting better with time by being exposed to increasing amounts of data.

Chapter 6: Data Science

As big data and computer science converged both in the development of new and more powerful hardware and storage systems and with the improved development of machine learning systems and artificial intelligence, a new field that is having a large impact on business intelligence was developed. This field is commonly known as data science. Data science is an interdisciplinary subject that brings together three different fields of study. These include computer science, statistics and probability, and business acumen. All three fields lie at the intersection of business intelligence and big data. In this chapter, we are going to get a handle on the field of data science and how it's going to be used with business intelligence in the future.

Data and Machines in Business

It might look obvious in hindsight, but when the Internet was invented, it increased the capability of companies to track people. No one could have predicted the way that this would merged with artificial intelligence and statistics in order to drive a new direction in technology. What the emergence of big data did was to bring together many different fields of study and their application in the real world in a new and different way.

In some ways – and for a while - machine learning was a solution looking for a problem. Big data has provided the exact type of problem that machine learning needs in order to work its magic. This marriage is part of what helps create the new field of data science. This is because a large part of the big data that has been generated is contained within the business environment. Therefore, a new need emerged for people with skill sets that would contain knowledge and abilities across multiple fields. In other words, traditionally computer scientists are not people who have business knowledge. In the old world, computer scientists would have been people whose skillset was focused on machine learning and artificial intelligence along with computer programming.

Then on the other side, you would have experts in the business. Businesspeople, including those trained formally in business school, were not the type of people that would have expertise in fields like machine learning. Therefore, they would not be able to even conceive of applying artificial intelligence to solving business problems, including incorporating it within the business intelligence structure.

In addition to all of this, there is a third subset of experts. That is the people from the mathematics realm who are experts in statistics and probability. These people are certainly able to apply their skillsets to a wide variety of problems. But, traditionally speaking, they have not been involved in the study and application of artificially intelligent computer systems.

The advent of big data has changed all this. The first problem began when businesses were collecting myriads of data, but they had no way to do anything with it. It soon became clear that the use of machine learning was the key to solving the big data problem. After the turn of the 21st-century, machine learning began to grow in importance in the use of dealing with big data in the context of business.

This created a new set of needs. Companies that were using big data began to develop a need for expertise across fields, people who could work with machine learning and artificial intelligence applications. These specialists were not needed to make them work, but to understand how to apply them within the business. These people would also need a thorough knowledge of statistics and probability in order to work with the systems, train the systems, and understand the results that they were producing. In order to do that, the expert would have to have B/business knowledge in addition to their other skillsets.

As these things converged, the field of data science was born, and it quickly became official.

Comparing and Contrasting Data Science and Business Intelligence

In the section, we need to revisit the definitions that are used for business intelligence and data science. First, let's look at what business intelligence is in relation to data. We must admit to ourselves that there is a's definition of business intelligence that is rooted in the past and that it needs to change as we keep evolving in a new situational environment. The main purpose of business intelligence has been to gather the current state of data that is behind the operation of the business for humans to make data-driven business decisions. Although recent efforts have been upgrading traditional business intelligence systems - such as data dashboards - for the most part, business intelligence is rooted in the static view of the business. In short, business intelligence looks at a frozen passed state of the business in order to move forward with new decision-making. This is a completely understandable situation, given the nature of the tools that have been available to businesses in the past. Large databases, and spreadsheets, and so forth, are - by their very nature - rooted in a static picture that is a snapshot of a past state of the data. Therefore, the process of business intelligence is to interpret the past data that has come into the business, and most of that data (if not all that data) has been in the form of structured data. Traditionally speaking business intelligence has been used to drive reporting or the development of spreadsheets which can present data in charts and so forth, that the business can use to interpret and then make decisions about future actions. This type of data has not been used to make predictive decisions for the most part.

So now let's look at what data science is, and how it operates. What we have done so far is to define the major components of data science that are used as tools. Those are machine learning, or artificial intelligence, business knowledge, and statistics. But these are tools, and they should not be confused with data science itself. Data science, like business intelligence, is a data-driven enterprise. However, data science looks to extract hidden patterns, meanings, and insights, from structured AND unstructured data. One of the key differences between data science and business intelligence is that data science seeks to either predict future outcomes or to be able to take advantage of unknown patterns in future data.

The naïve observer would look at this and believe that business intelligence and data science are completely different. They seem to have different goals, and they're applied to different situations. They do have some things in common on the surface. That is, both data science and business intelligence are looking to improve the competitive advantages of the enterprise. This can be done across the entire operational procedures of the business. It can impact the allocation of resources, customer service, expansion into markets, increasing efficiency and avoiding wasteful spending, and other things that impact the general efficiency and success of the business. Thus, everyone will agree that to a certain extent, data science and business intelligence can have the same end goals for the company in mind.

However, one should step back and look at what business intelligence really is. The fact is, business intelligence is going to grow and evolve in this new environment, and it will incorporate data science into the business intelligence model and process and use it to help drive not only increasing efficiency, but also actionable decision-making. It is not necessary for upper-level management and senior executives to have detailed understandings about the workings of data science. It is up to the data science team to extract useful information from their activities that can be used for important decision-making by upper-level executives.

It is also a myth that business intelligence must be constrained to using structured data. Data science represents an opportunity to expand business intelligence into a broader framework that can utilize the huge amounts of unstructured data that companies are collecting both externally and internally. We have already described the ways that unstructured information that a company has access to could be used to improve the efficiency of the company massively. Think about what some of the end goals are business intelligence when it comes to using the data that it does use in a traditional sense. The problem that most analysts have had when it comes to looking at business intelligence is there to focus on the sources of the data in the way that they are presented and utilized by the business. Instead, you should focus on the end results that you would seek to achieve through the application of business intelligence. When you do this, it is easier to adopt a broader horizon within which you can incorporate the tools and sources of data used in data science.

Let's take a concrete example from UPS. It is well known that UPS utilized Machine learning systems in order to identify patterns exhibited by their drivers during day-to-day operations. From this effort, the company was able to identify changes that could be made to reduce fuel consumption across the company. These changes were then implemented. So, if we ignore the source of the data, we can see that this is the kind of problem that we might address using business intelligence, if only we had the information available. The only difference here is one of technology. That is in a traditional sense; the type of data needed to solve this problem simply was not available using the tools that have been traditionally in existence when it comes to Business intelligence. But you can read any business intelligence book or article and find copious examples of how one of the goals of business intelligence is to improve operations in the business — furthermore, decisions made using business intelligence our data-driven decisions. So, looking at the UPS example, where is the distinction between what the data is telling you and then making a data-driven decision based on it, or saying it is data science or business intelligence?

The reality here is that we are looking out data science in the wrong way. Instead of seeing data science as a distinct entity, we should instead view data science as an additional tool that can be used as part of the overall process of business intelligence. Too many people who are experts in business intelligence are making these mistakes because they are uneducated or lack proper education when it comes to data science. Quite frankly, the understanding of many business intelligence experts of data science is confined to a top-level understanding of it that they glean from reading articles and publications. In fact, we can go so far as to say that some people in the business intelligence community are threatened by data science.

However, when you step back and look at how data science can be used, it's clear that these fears are completely misplaced. There is absolutely no reason for the business intelligence community to try to keep data science outside of it or to even fear it. Instead, it should be embraced and incorporated into the totality of business intelligence.

You will read articles about business intelligence that claim that it can only understand data that is structured and formatted. That is completely absurd. It is limited thinking that is only viewing business intelligence than the framework of current technologies. Buy an analogy, let's imagine that it's 1975, and the issue is the introduction of electronic computers together with word processors and spreadsheets. If we were using the logic that some in the business intelligence community are using now, you would have said that spreadsheets could play no role in the accounting department, because accountants are working with pencil and paper ledgers. But what happened as spreadsheets were adopted? The accounting process changed and incorporated spreadsheets within it.

This is what is going to happen when it comes to the relationship between business intelligence and data science. The reason that this is going to happen is that data science and business intelligence have the same goals when it comes to meeting the needs of improving the competitive advantages of the business. Furthermore, both data science and business intelligence seek to promote data-based decision-making.

Also, you should not get caught up in the situation of focusing on the fact that in many cases, artificial intelligence systems are able to work autonomously. That is another side issue that only serves as a distraction. Again, I refer you back to the earlier two examples provided (UPS and Southwest Airlines), which were able to make very important decisions that improved the efficiencies of their businesses while saving hundreds of millions of dollars. In both cases, this was done using machine learning and data science. It is clear to this author that looking at the results they could be considered to be something that would fit within the overarching realm of business intelligence if you're willing to expand it and update the notion of what business intelligence is going forward into the future.

Improved Efficiency Through Automation

Remember the V's that we talked about regarding big data? One of the V's was volume, and another was velocity. These two are going to increase exponentially as the years and decades pass. That means businesses are going to be forced into a situation where they need to rely on data science and data scientists in order to interpret and understand the big data that is playing a role in their business.

The intern is going to be increasingly influenced by artificial intelligence and autonomous computer systems. This is only going to serve to increase the efficiency of business intelligence massively. Many aspects of business intelligence that are traditionally done by humans are going to be increasingly automated and made far more efficient. That is going to magnify the power of business intelligence exponentially. It is going to be an incumbent on business intelligence experts to bring themselves up to speed on data science; they will have to increase their understanding of statistics and machine intelligence.

This requirement is often misunderstood and often framed in terms of an either/or situation. That is, we are returning to the view that business intelligence is somehow threatened by data science. But once again, this is a complete misunderstanding. Rather than looking at data science as being competitive to business intelligence and making excuses about people in business intelligence not understanding or being able to understand the workings of data science, we need to be realistic about this. Does someone in business intelligence understand all the computer code that is behind a database, or the internal workings of spreadsheet programs like Microsoft Excel?

Of course not. What they do understand is the high-level aspects of these tools. So, when it comes to incorporating data science into business intelligence, a high-level understanding of the tools is what is necessary. In this way, data science is going to enhance the ability of those in business intelligence to make it effective and actionable decisions for the business. Once again, we have already seen how this works in practice. Data science is helping companies improve their efficiency, break into new markets, allocate resources effectively, massively expand, and improve their marketing, advertising, customer service, and much more. Let's look at some potential applications a big data and data science that can have exciting uses within the context of better business intelligence.

Until recently, and even in the present for most companies, huge amounts of useful data that can improve internal operations are simply sitting collecting dust on hard drives. Companies need to analyze ways that employees are communicating with each other and using their time in order to improve efficiency.

We are starting to see this with monitoring systems based on artificial intelligence. Companies are so much as snooping, because you are working on company time, and the organization has every right to see how their employees are using their time and resources. For those companies that have started using these tools, increasing the level of productivity and efficiency among employees has been one of the many benefits to come out of this. It makes it easier to weed out bad employees and makes it possible to bring problems to the attention of good employees, allowing those employees to rectify the situation. By studying the movements of employees, it's also possible to reallocate the positioning of employees in the company to increase the efficiency of collaboration between different groups and employees. This is analogous to views of artificial intelligence in hospital environments wherein nursing staff has been completely redesigned to consider the needs of patients throughout the facilities. So, in the same way, a company that really doesn't understand why it distributes employees among offices the way it does can instead put employees in locations where they are going to be needed most of the time. Until now, the tenancy has been to distribute employees in the building based on the group or department they belong in, considering where any free office space exists. What if instead, you actually studied the data derived from tracking employee movements where they were spending most of their time that was devoted to productive activity and then you brought employees closer together that actually needed to be close together in order to get work done?

Self-Service BI

Earlier, we mentioned that one of the capabilities of artificial intelligence systems is that they can work autonomously without human input. One of the developments that are coming out of this is the idea of self-service business intelligence platforms. This will allow companies to increase efficiency as far as incorporating business intelligence throughout the organization. It will be easier for those who need business intelligence services to get it exactly when they need it. Furthermore, it can help companies become more efficient by reducing staffing requirements.

In addition, artificial intelligence systems can learn, and they will continue to learn and become better at what they do the more they are used. Every time an artificially intelligent or self-service business intelligence system is used, the machine is learning and improving itself in response to new data that is coming in. What does this mean for the business? It means that it will have business intelligence that is consistently improving itself autonomously. Furthermore, artificial intelligence systems can work 24/7 without becoming tired or complaining. As time goes on, this is going to mean that self-service business intelligence platforms are going to grow in power exponentially. This is only going to help the business skyrocket its efficiency and productivity.

Labor Saving

Another benefit of incorporating machine learning and business intelligence is that just like using machines and other contexts, data science is going to free up human labor that can then be used for other purposes. Unfortunately, far too many people are completely misreading this situation. Instead of looking at it as the opportunity that it is, they are viewing it with fear. It is rather disconcerting to see large numbers of smart people who giving in to the old Luddite philosophy that has been proven wrong repeatedly throughout history. For some reason, these people are viewing the tools of data science and artificial intelligence as somehow different than other machines, including computers applied in different circumstances.

What's important to understand about this is the fact that the nature of the machine being used is not the relevant factor here. This is because when human beings are freed from labor, they invent entirely new things to do, things that they didn't imagine anyone would want to do *before the changes came into existence*. There are many examples of this that have taken place since the development of computers. For example, one of the most popular activities on iPhones and iPads is playing solitaire. If you were able to travel back in time and ask someone in 1960 whether people would want to play solitaire or poker on the phone, they would have looked at you as if you were completely crazy!

Now consider one of these side effects that is occurred as a result of people playing games like this on their phones. This has created a massive business that didn't exist before 2008, devoted entirely to developing games that can be played on mobile phones. This industry is developing so rapidly and growing so fast that in just ten years it has grown into a multibillion-dollar industry that employs hundreds of thousands of people directly, and hundreds of thousands of additional contractors.

Even if you went back to the year 2005, such a scenario might've been deemed impossible.

The point of the story is that new technology leads to unexpected developments that increase the employability of people. Yes, they need to learn new skills. Before 2008, there probably weren't many people that knew how to create a card game on a mobile phone.

Likewise, as business intelligence becomes more automated (and to a certain extent more dominated by data science0, that doesn't mean that the people in business intelligence are going to have to go on unemployment. What it is likely to mean is that businesses are going to find new and unexpected ways that business intelligence can and will be used in order to improve the performance and competitive advantages of the business. Therefore, my prediction is that ten years from now there are going to be more people employed in business intelligence than there are now.

Let's look at one of the final benefits of incorporating data science into business intelligence. By automating more tasks that are associated with business intelligence and increasing the role of unstructured data, this is going to free up the enterprise so that it can focus on goals and outcomes rather than on tedious tasks and efforts to interpret data. Data interpretation is going to be made far more efficient and productive as a result of these improvements.

So, this leads one to believe that data science is going to help massively improve the outputs that result from the use of business intelligence while also increasing the efficiency of business intelligence. Rather than looking at data science and business intelligence as being in conflict or at best as having an application into distinct realms, we should instead focus on the fact that these two fields are going to merge and be complementary. Later, as the tools and results of data science begin to seem natural, you might even start viewing data science and business intelligence as being two sides of the same coin.

When it comes to developing and maintaining a competitive advantage for your business, there is no question in my mind that you're going to need to incorporate both data science and business intelligence together in order to survive the future hyper-competitive environment. If you are not doing so, I can guarantee that your competitors *will* be doing it.

Chapter 7: Cybersecurity

At the foundation of business intelligence, we find data. This data is in many forms and may be stored in many different locations. We have seen that businesses include a lot of structured data that may be stored internally on their own computer servers. It is accessed in the form of relational databases, spreadsheets, and other data structures. Companies are also collecting and storing a lot of unstructured, internal data as well as data from customers and external sources that may have unstructured formats. All this data represents key components of the business operation. It is important for the business to maintain the security and integrity of this data. As a result, cybersecurity is going to be playing an increasing role in the future of business intelligence. If the data that a company has is not secure, then business intelligence is not going to be operating at the level it should.

Determining Infosec Needs of the Company

Cybersecurity is going to be involved with business intelligence in multiple ways. One of the ways that it's going to be involved is that upper-level management and security teams are always going to need to be able to evaluate the security of their data. This is one area where Machine intelligence and data science can play a central role. Machine intelligence can be used not only to secure data but also to identify and present security weaknesses that exist in the organization. It will be up to the management teams to determine what to do with this information. However, there's no question that using the capabilities of machine learning weaknesses that can be exploited and other to threaten the company and the security of its data is going to be identified in unexpected and new ways. This is only going to serve to improve and enhance the ability of the company to respond to information security threats as they arise.

So, what we are envisioning in this context is using machine learning in order to identify threats that exist for the information that is so vital to the company's competitive advantages. This fits in well with business intelligence for several reasons. The most significant reason is that it will enable involved management concerned with information security to make data-driven actionable decisions. Of course, these decisions are going to be involved with the usual kinds of trade-offs that businesses always face, such as practicality considerations and cost-effectiveness.

Cybersecurity in a nutshell

At this point, let's look at what cybersecurity involves. In today's world, many of the key components of the business include software applications, computer systems, computer networks, and data. These systems are in constant threat from malicious actors throughout the world. One of the side effects of the internet that we may not like is that malicious actors, located anywhere, are able to locate, detect, an attack any computer system that they choose. An interesting aspect of these malicious actors is that although a lot of the news is focused on large-scale hacking attacks, it is often small businesses that are the targets of these kinds of efforts.

Let's look at some of the types of attacks and how they occur. The most common that people focus on is a hacking attack which breaks into a computer system for the purpose of stealing data. This is a classic case of breaking into a large business computer system in order to get the names and Social Security numbers of people that hold credit cards.

However, there are many other types of attacks that can occur. For example, you can imagine that some unethical people would like to deal with competitive threats not by stealing people's credit card numbers, but instead by tampering with the data that a company has. Throughout the book, we have discussed the importance of data that is becoming critical for company operations. Think about how you could damage a company by breaking into their computer network and not stealing anything, but rather tampering with the data. If this attack went undetected, that data would be used for all kinds of purposes. All the machine learning and analysis that we've been talking about would be continuing based on tampered data that might even be fake. The company would be led down the road to making bad decisions based on bad data.

When it comes to small-scale attacks, ransomware is a common threat. This is used to extract - or at least - attempt to get money from victims.

As time goes on, all the above attacks and more are becoming increasingly sophisticated. There's basically an arms race going on between the cybersecurity community and malicious actors worldwide. Interestingly, many of these malicious actors are not individuals or teenagers working out of their mother's basement. In fact, many countries such as China, Iran, Russia, and North Korea, have official government programs that promote hacking attempts and cyber espionage. Considering that in some of these countries - especially China – many corporations are state-owned or partially state-owned, it doesn't seem far-fetched to imagine that they would not be above tampering with data of competitors in other countries.

The Approach to Cybersecurity

Modern approaches to cybersecurity are based on a five-step process. This includes identifying threats, protection from threats, detection of threats, repeat and refine.

Identifying and detecting threats is increasingly coming under the domain of machine learning. This was one of the earliest applications of machine learning which had a practical use. By using anomaly detection and classification algorithms, machine learning systems can detect attempts to break into a network that are probably malicious in intent. Many computer systems are under constant attack and the ability of machine learning systems to adapt while spotting anomalous behavior makes them well-suited to playing a central role in cybersecurity.

Data Science and Cybersecurity

Big data has a large role to play when it comes to cybersecurity. By utilizing big data, it is possible to find trends in the underlying data related to cybersecurity. This can be used to determine patterns of attacks that are made. It is impossible to know what those patterns are going to be ahead of time; however, you can look for things such as attacks during certain time frames. Once that is determined, it can turn from a raw piece of data into actionable Intel.

Data science can only help with this process. One of the ways that it can assist with an actionable intel is that it's going to be possible to use unstructured machine learning in order to detect unexpected patterns, relationships, trends, that exist in relation to attacks on computer networks and systems. For example, a machine learning system may detect the most likely times of day, departments, or even computer terminals that are most likely to be used in an attack. When this information is known to the security team, this is data that can be used in order to make actionable business decisions to increase the security of the company.

Another way the data science can be used together with machine learning is to develop more secure systems. That is rather than having humans develop new login systems or encryption, you can put the task to artificially intelligent systems. They are more likely to develop protocols that are hard to break and add more security. One of the ways that they're going to be able to do this is that you can train the machine learning systems by giving them data over the past history of the organization and the computer networks that the system can learn from in order to detect patterns of attack and also understand the types of attack that the system is most likely to encounter.

Big data is going to relate to cybersecurity in two different ways. We have already determined that big data can be used to train machine learning systems to understand the patterns and past practices that have been used by malicious actors in order to try and break into the computer networks. However, big data is also a liability. For many companies, it is the presence of all the data they hold in the first place – that cache of information is making them subject to attack. If we are going to say that data is the gold of the 21st-century, it makes perfect sense that people the world over are going to try in access that data in malicious and illegal ways. So, the more data of the company has, the more important cybersecurity is going to be to the organization.

By utilizing big data and machine intelligence and cybersecurity, businesses will be able to develop more accurate and effective defense systems against attack on their computer networks. In addition, this type of information can be incorporated into business intelligence and help management develop more cost-effective solutions. In other words, management will be able to maximize cybersecurity while keeping budgets at the most efficient levels possible. They will be able to precisely target where money needs to go in order to maximize cybersecurity going into the future year.

The Three Tenets of Cybersecurity

It is often said that cybersecurity is based on three tenets that are called the"

"CIA triad". Maybe the name is a little bit unfortunate. In any case, C stands for *confidentiality*. Confidentiality measures are used within cybersecurity to protect data from unauthorized access. This is one area where clear application the big data together with machine learning can be used to make confidentiality protections better.

The second area of cybersecurity is *integrity*. We have mentioned this earlier. There is a good reason for malicious actors, especially if they come from other companies or nationally directed enterprises to tamper with data rather than expose it. Integrity is the component of cybersecurity that would protect data from unauthorized changes. The types of changes that could be used include changing the data itself. That kind of attack would ripple throughout the enterprise. So, this is a very serious part of cybersecurity. Data also must be protected from unauthorized access that would add new data up to the datasets or delete data.

The third tenet of cybersecurity is *availability*. It is important for cybersecurity to function in a way that is basically running in the background. It can't interfere with the normal operations of the company. Users in the business are always going to need to access data practically already keep the company running at peak efficiency. Therefore, availability is going to be important for those in cybersecurity to consider.

Threat Detection

Of course, one of the most important aspects of cybersecurity is going to be threat detection when there are attacks on the network and attempts at unauthorized access. In order to work best, this type of threat detection must be operating in real-time. This is not something that humans are well-suited to do. You can immediately draw the conclusion that this is a task that would be best propose for artificially intelligent systems. In fact, you won't be surprised to learn that machine learning is applied to this very task all the time. Threat detection is a simple task for machine learning systems, if you have the data necessary for them to learn on. By presenting machine learning systems with past data of attacks on computer networks, they're able to learn and spot anomalous behavior that would indicate an unauthorized access attempt of the network. Businesses and organizations may be, to some extent, better off if they do this type of analysis on their own if they can do so. The reason is that attacks directed at a company may be unique in nature to a certain extent. For small businesses, they may have to rely on off-the-shelf software products. These products will still be very effective because they have been trained in a wide range of possible cybersecurity threats.

Chapter 8: BI and Data Mining

The core idea behind business intelligence is to use the data that a business has available in order to develop actionable information. This will help the business operate more efficiently because management will be able to make data-driven decisions rather than trying to act on incomplete information and hunches. As it stands on its own, data is not useful in its raw form. This is where business intelligence comes in. It is going to take that data and make it in a form that can be presentable two human beings that can then make informed decisions based on what the data is telling them.

As such, business intelligence will pull together all the data in the organization, analyze the data, present that data in report form or in a visualized way, which will make the data meaningful for management. Then in order to enhance the competitiveness and efficiency of the business, management can make data-driven decisions.

Data Mining

Now let's become more acquainted with data mining. Data mining is a jargon word in a sense. It already has a lot in common with some of the things we've been discussing. The first thing that data mining is involved in is *large datasets*. In other words, here we have big data yet again – but that is only in first appearances. In fact, part of data mining is "mining" the data, finding smaller subsets within the large datasets that are useful for the analytical purposes at hand.

Another thing the data mining is involved in is recognizing hidden patterns that exist in these large datasets. Thus, we are back to the tasks that are carried out with machine learning, although this isn't explicitly specified when discussing data mining. Data mining attempts to classify and categorize data so that it's more useful to the organization.

So, we start with raw data which is basically useless. Data mining helps convert that data into something that can provide value as far as the information that it contains. A part of data mining is going to be selecting the data that you want to use. Data warehousing is an important foundation upon which data mining is based. Companies need to be able to store and access data in large amounts which is why data warehousing with effective solutions that are fast and accurate is important. Then the data must go through a cleansing process. That is when you have huge amounts of data, one of the problems that you're going to an encounter is that data is going to be often corrupted or missing. This is something that is very common when it comes to relational databases, but this can also happen when you're restoring huge amounts of unstructured data.

After the data has been gathered, extracted, and cleansed, the process of data mining moves on to look for the patterns needed to gather useful information from the data. Once this is done, the data can be used in many ways by a business. For example, it could be used for sales analysis or for customer management and service. Data mining has also been used for fraud detection. There is much of overlap between data mining and other activities involving big data, such as machine learning. When it comes to data mining, you're going to see a lot of statistical analysis.

This intelligence and data mining are both involved in the process of converting raw data into actionable information for the business. However, the goal of business intelligence is to present data in meaningful ways so that management can make data-driven decisions. In contrast, data mining is used to find solutions to existing problems.

If you remember when we talked about big data, one of the things that were important was volume. Business intelligence is certainly driven by large datasets. However, data mining is different in this respect. Relevant data is going to be extracted from the raw data to be used in data mining. Therefore, relatively speaking, data mining is going to be working with smaller subsets of the data that is available. This is one characteristic that is going to separate data mining from the other topics that we have talked about so far. Data mining might be used as a part of an overall strategy of business intelligence. So, what management is looking for from data mining is solutions that can be applied to business intelligence. This contrasts with business intelligence on its own, as it is usually used to present data to people.

So, the core result obtained from data mining is knowledge. This is in the form of a solution that can be applied within business intelligence. This provides a big advantage to business and operations. That is because the findings from data mining can be applied rapidly within business intelligence.

Data mining is also a tool within business intelligence that allows business intelligence to extract complex data, presenting it understandable forms that are useful for the people in the organization. The data extracted with data mining can be presented in readable reports or in graphical format containing graphs and charts. In this form, it becomes a part of business intelligence so that the people in the organization can understand, better interpreting the data and making actionable decisions based on that data.

The volume of data coming to large businesses is only growing with time. This makes both data mining and business intelligence more important to the organization as the onslaught of information continues to pour in. It is going to be important to cull the data in terms of saliency; this is where data mining plays a role. The data is always changing, making this task even more important. Demand for data mining and business intelligence solutions will be increased in proportion to the growth of the volume of data.

For companies to remain competitive and - especially if they want to be a market leader - they are going to have to utilize data mining and business intelligence solutions for retaining their advantages.

Data Analytics

Data is not useful if you cannot draw conclusions from it. Data analytics is a process of organizing and examining datasets for the purpose of extracting useful and actionable information from the data. Data analytics plays a role in business intelligence, using tools like OLAP for reporting and analytical processing. When done effectively, data analytics can help a business become more competitive and efficient, build better and more targeted marketing campaigns, improve customer service, and meet the goals that are a part of business intelligence. Data analytics can be applied to any data that an organization has access to, including internal and external sources of data. It can use old data or even real-time data to provide more readable information that can be accessed by employees in the organization in an effective way to help them make actionable decisions.

While data analytics can be used as a part of business intelligence efforts, like machine learning, data analytics can be used for *predictive modeling*, which is not part of business intelligence. Typically, BI is used for an informed decision-making process based on analytics of past data. Data analytics uses past data but can apply it with predictive analytics to help the company use modeling and tools to determine future directions of various efforts that can help the company maintain its edge and advance even further.

Data analytics will also be used in many ways that are like processing data with machine learning. That is, it will be useful for pattern recognition, prediction, and cluster analysis. Data analytics is also an important part of the data mining process.

Chapter 9: BI and Social Media

Over the past year, the data collection powers of the social media companies have come to the forefront of many discussions. At the top of the list of concerns is privacy. Regardless of what you think about these discussions, one thing is clear: social media has resulted in the collection of unprecedented amounts of data - not only about individual people but also about businesses that use these platforms. Social media is a very effective way to collect data on customers.

Social media represents unprecedented opportunities for businesses. For one thing, social media will help businesses understand the behavior of their customers. Social media also helps businesses target the market to new customers and acquire them. It also provides an opportunity for a business to put their face forward in new ways.

In this chapter, we are going to look at the power of social media in terms of interaction between business intelligence and social media; we will explore how that can help businesses expand and improve their competitive advantage.

Leveraging Social Media

There are many ways that a business can leverage social media. The first way is to recognize that companies like Facebook and Twitter have an imaginable treasure trove of data on every customer. The data collected is thorough and global. Moreover, companies like Facebook are ahead in terms of organizing that data and putting it into a useful form. So, the existence of social media companies not only provides a platform through which a business can increase awareness, but it has also created an environment where other companies are doing a lot of the hard work for you. So, there's a bonanza cache of unstructured data that is not only being stored by companies like Facebook, it is also being analyzed. So, let's begin at the beginning: the first advantage that we have here is that we don't have to worry about storage capacity because Facebook or Google already has that data stored for us.

This data has also been put into a form that makes it friendly for all kinds of analysis. And although there is a lot of hype about privacy violations, the facts show that for the most part, data is presented in aggregate ways, preventing the targeting of any individuals *unless those individuals voluntarily choose to interact with other companies.* "Voluntarily choose" means that an individual has freely given their name and email address to the company for its use – and has read, understood, and agreed to the company's privacy policies.

Web Scraping Tools

Web scraping tools allow a company to obtain data that is on other websites (publicly available data) without having to copy and paste it manually. These types of tools allow businesses to get data from social media sites that can then be analyzed and used. This data will be in an unstructured form, and as such, will be well suited for analysis using machine learning. No matter which social media platform you are scraping data from, you are going to have mixed data in almost every case. Consider a Facebook post as an example. A Facebook post may have an image associated with it, but it might be plain text. It could also include a video. It might have a hyperlink and emojis. So, there is a mixture of data that is contained in one single object. This is also true on many other social media platforms; while Pinterest and Instagram are photo platforms (primarily), postings will have text, hashtags, and possibly hyperlinks.

In order to get usable information with this data, it must be rigorously "percolated" via a data grinder. As we mentioned, this is clearly big data, and it's also unstructured data. That means it is not particularly well suited for use in traditional business intelligence, but rather must be processed using big data and machine learning methods. You will also be searching for hidden patterns in the data. As an example, if you were looking for a hyperlink appearing in many Facebook posts, you would need to cross-link it with the people that are posting the link in order to find their demographics.

Web scraping might seem like an insurmountable task, but it can have many advantages. It provides a way to collect data that can be used for marketing research. It can also be used to extract contact information. However, the value of doing that is questionable, as most people don't respond well to contacts that they – themselves – have not initiated.

There are many effective web scraping tools that are available. You can consider using import.io, dexi.io, and visual scraper. These powerful tools can help you do some pre-processing on the data, assisting you in retrieving the desired type of data that are useful for your purposes. In some cases, you might be able to get it into a form that can be directly used in business intelligence.

Direct Interaction with Customers

One of the interesting benefits of social media is that it provides businesses with the ability to interact with customers directly. This is going to involve some effort on the part of the business; the more effort that is put in, the more likely it is going to pay off. And the fact is, this is easy to maintain, and can be done on a low budget. In the following chapter, we will be discussing the types of advertising that can take your direct interaction with customers to a new level.

The first step toward direct interaction with customers is to create a Facebook page for the business. A Facebook page is essentially like a Facebook profile, but they are created either for group interests, hobbies, or in the case of interest to us businesses. The Facebook page is going to have a timeline and a photo repository, just like any normal Facebook profile would. One of the mistakes that a lot of businesses are making: they create Facebook pages, but then fail to maintain them. If you're a small business, it's vitally important that you maintain the Facebook page. It doesn't take a lot of work, and one or two posts per day are enough to grow the Facebook page over time.

Unfortunately, what you often see when visiting Facebook pages for businesses is very few posts at all, and many just create the page and leave it there as a placeholder. Among those that do post, they don't do so effectively. Your post must be engaging, inviting users to comment on and share the post. As we will learn in the next chapter, we can use advertising to bring in more users.

But the main benefits of the Facebook page are that once somebody likes the page, your posts will start showing up on *their timeline!* This is only one of the many benefits of marketing by posting regularly on a Facebook page: when your posts are shared, it creates a domino effect! Friends of the person who originally shared will see your post, and they may share, and then - you get the picture! By posting interesting, engaging content, you are reaching far more people than just those who happen to see your post in the first place.

A side point to note: user comments left by viewers on your Facebook page are data. Even if you are running a small-scale operation, these comments can be analyzed by those at your company, providing actionable information.

The Challenges of Social Media

As a business, one of the challenges of social media is determining which platforms are the most useful for the purposes of your business. The first factor to consider is the question: what are your main customer demographics? There are certain social media platforms that are used more frequently by young people, whereas other social media platforms are used by the general public. The form of data on social media platforms may also vary from platform to platform.

Let's get started by looking at a few examples. One of the most popular social media platforms (and one that does not get much press) is Pinterest. This platform has been around for a while, and although it has a mobile app now, its original introduction to the public was as a website. This website's purpose is to share user images, and its primary audience in female. Of course, that doesn't mean that males are not on the website; however, in proportional terms, the audience tends to be female, and more specifically, it tends to be females of a certain age groups. It is estimated that the age group of 18-30 makes up most active users on Pinterest.

Let's contrast this information with that of Facebook and its users. Facebook has been around for a long time, becoming dominant around ten years ago. The advantage of Facebook is that most people already use it in a personal manner, so the audience is already vast. If you are targeting Facebook and looking for the advantages, the biggest one is already baked in you are going to be able to reach nearly every demographic that there is! If you are using social media to leverage people over the age of 50, Facebook works for you. It would also work perfectly fine if your customer demographic was 18 to 34.

Now let's look at Instagram, which is owned by Facebook. Instagram is an app-only interface. This fact alone probably makes it more appealing to younger people. Although Instagram has recently become used more by older people, it remains primarily the

18 to 34 age group. Gender is more balanced on Instagram as compared to Pinterest.

Twitter is another platform that, like Facebook, seems to appeal to all age groups. One downside of Twitter is that due to the nature of the platform's communication protocol, advertising on Twitter is a bit more difficult. Some businesses may have trouble connecting with users due to this flaw. That said, it has 600 million active users, and so it can *reach a lot of people.*

There are other social media platforms such as Snapchat and WhatsApp. These are confined to the mobile space and appeal mostly to people under the age of 30.

This is an incomplete review but helps to demonstrate that you need to choose your social media platforms carefully based on what your business is doing, as well as its demographics.

Data Issues with Social Media

Social media can present data in a wide variety of forms. One of the first factors that you need to consider is heterogeneity. This means we need to examine the data in terms of the *data types* included in social media postings. So, if heterogeneity is strong, it means that the data is taking many different forms. Think multimedia here. Data may be in the form of text, images, and video – or other types that you don't readily consider but may be extremely useful. For example, the hyperlinks that people put in their social media postings are going to tell you a lot about that person. Hashtags are also important to look at. As you can see, social media postings contain more data than meets the eye at first. By looking at hashtags, it may be possible to glean information such as political affiliation for things that the poster is interested in.

The viral nature of social media is also something to consider. One question you must ask: is a post by an individual an *original post*, or is it a *shared post*? Even if a person shares a post, it may still provide data about that person. More than likely, if the person shares a post, they either found it interesting or they share the views or interests that are present in the post. They may just think it's funny. These factors can present a challenge to businesses trying to do an analysis of social media data.

It is possible to retrieve data from social media sites using web scraping tools. That takes a lot of processing power, and how it handles and separates that data presents a difficult choice. Data will have to be sorted by source, and by type. Different types of analysis can be applied to the data once you have an in your possession. Clustering analysis could be very helpful. For example, you could consider looking at all the posts that share a particular link. Then an analysis could be used to determine the characteristics or other data points of the people that share the link. This can be important for marketing purposes, and it's even used by political professionals that are trying to target people that may be open to their messages.

Another issue related to social media data concerns immediacy. If you're going to utilize social media data, you are going to need to know how recent the data is. Data from five or ten years ago probably isn't going to be very relevant. The more immediate the data is, the more valuable the data is.

Second, social media provides huge amounts of data. This is the scaling problem. For organizations working with this data on their own, this can be an extremely difficult problem to deal with. This may force organizations to either: 1) have companies like Facebook do analysis on their behalf (probably the most efficient way to do it,) or 2) they can work with smaller datasets and try to do it themselves. That process, however, it's probably not as effective as it would be utilizing the power of the social media companies themselves in order to help your business.

What Can You Get from Social Media?

Let's take a step back and think about what we can get from social media. Social media offers unprecedented power that we can use to investigate the private lives of people. This is not to say that you should be snooping on people. We are talking about information that these people have voluntarily chosen to make publicly available. This information is extremely useful from a business perspective, allowing you to determine many things about different people, including interests, hobbies, and goals. People often list important information with their profile that can be combined with information such as age, gender, and birthplace. All this information can be combined and analyzed using machine learning capabilities in order to extract useful patterns for marketing purposes.

One of the keys to social media is you want to be able to speak directly to your consumers in ways that they can relate to. By analyzing data that is either shared by the social media company for you (or that you've scraped,) this will help you connect better with your customers.

Dashboarding the Data

One way that many businesses deal with data from social media companies is by using dashboards. So, for example, they can ask questions about people with different demographics. This information can be gathered from social media sites. In fact, Facebook provides a dashboard-like interface that you can use to analyze Facebook users in terms of many characteristics such as education, websites they have shown interest in, and more.

For larger organizations, it may possible to integrate social media data and develop internal data dashboards that can be used in order to access and analyze the data. For example, you can create clusters of users by various characteristics. You might be interested in males, ages 30 to 44, unmarried. Then you could use the data dashboard to extract different information about this demographic. This is all part of business intelligence.

Hopefully, you can see where this is going: the result is that we can create actionable information from these types of analyses.

Three Ways to Use Social Media

The businesses that have the most success with social media are those that understand the central premise of social media. Take a step back and think about what Facebook is about. The central theme of Facebook's connection. Put differently, social media is about building relationships. This means that there are going to be three ways that a business can utilize and exploit social media.

The first way is to build relationships with your client base. This can include active clients as well as prospective ones. That is one reason why you should create and maintain a Facebook page and actively engage with the people that post there. This will go a long way two getting your company to build relationships with the customers. You want to make it personal and real. People have a certain type of radar that they can use on a subconscious level to detect whether something is genuine or not. This is not to say that people are not possible to fool; of course, they are - Bernie Madoff proved that! Even so, people do have a certain sense of these sorts of things. Businesses should go into social media with the intent of being genuine and building real relationships with people. Even if a company is a large organization, it would benefit by putting an actual face to the page. So, it might be possible to have an employee who is dedicated to running Facebook pages and interacting with customers.

The second way that social media can be utilized includes what we have been discussing up to this point: data gathering. This is the first step to incorporate social media data into your business intelligence. From there, they can be analyzed using the tools that you already have. The applications of using this data are going to depend on your business needs and the reasons that you're collecting this data. It might be to get a picture of the ideal customer. This is a very powerful way of marketing if you can get an idea of who the ideal customer is. Alternatively, you may be breaking things down, using clustering in order to determine what different groups are driven by in terms of their interests and desires. This will help you market to different groups using targeted methods that are going to speak more directly to them.

In summary, social media can help you develop more effective relationships with consumers and more effective marketing tools. The way that this information should be used is to communicate directly to users in a way that touches them directly and strikes a sensitive chord in them.

Third, you are going to want to use social media to put your advertising and marketing efforts on steroids. This is a topic that we are going to discuss in the next chapter.

Chapter 10: BI and Internet Marketing

When it comes to marketing and business intelligence, there has never been a more powerful era for companies. The seemingly endless data streams that are available for businesses allow them to market in unprecedented ways. People have been noticing this, watching artificially intelligent driven systems customize advertising for each individual person using the Internet. Many people find this annoying, but the truth is that it *works very well for business*.

Even if you're running a small business, there are many tools that you can leverage in order to elevate your internet marketing efforts. Facebook has moved to the forefront of Internet marketing and is a very powerful player in the space. But you should not limit your approaches to advertising and marketing online to Facebook alone. In this chapter, we are going to explore issues around internet marketing and business intelligence.

Social Media and Internet Platforms Best Suited for Online Marketing

Let's begin by giving an overview of some of the social media and Internet platforms that are best suited to effective Internet marketing.

When it comes to internet marketing, given all the data that is available, you want to think in terms of laser targeting and focus. In fact, one of the mistakes that some advertisers are making is there advertising the old way. What do we mean by that? The old way to market was to simply throw things out there and hope that the right people see it and act based on the advertisement. With all the data that is available today, that is a bad approach to take to marketing.

Let's look at a specific example. You can browse general websites, and they often have a lot of advertisements on them. Consider CNN as one example. You might think that advertising on CNN is a great thing to do. After all, they have huge numbers of eyeballs on the website all the time; people are constantly checking for the latest news. However, unless you have a business that is oriented toward the general public at large, advertising on a website like that is going to be a waste of money and time. The reason is that a small fraction of the audience is going to be interested in your product or service. For the most part, you're going to be spending precious dollars to put an ad in front of people that don't care about your services or product. In fact, most of them are never going to care about your company! Why would you want to spend dollars doing that? Spending money on untargeted advertising is a poor choice when you can use other services to put your ads right in front of the people who want your product!

However, there are exceptions to this. Many times, after you have looked at a product on one web page, you'll soon discover that suddenly ads are popping up for that product on other websites you browse. For instance, you are considering a new dog food on Chewy.com, but when you leave that site and start browsing other sites, you begin to see promotional ads for dog food on the sidebars. When a company starts using this type of targeted internet advertising, better results are seen, and more people are reached for your specific product or service. This type of marketing and advertising is driven by artificial intelligence.

Another factor to consider is cost. It turns out that advertising on social media platforms can be dirt cheap. You can start advertising on Facebook in order to do testing of advertisements for as little as five dollars a day. No, of course, you're not going to advertise at that lower level if you're looking to scale your business to reach large numbers of customers. Still, you would be surprised at how effective this is for testing ads to determine which ones are going to work or not.

So, we've already identified Facebook as a perfect marketing platform. Facebook lets you finely your advertisements to the specific demographics most interested in your product, service, or business. Another advantage of Facebook marketing is that you are going to be able to collect a lot of data in the process. The data that you collect with Facebook marketing is going to be something that you can use later to make your advertising efforts even more focused. Don't forget the case study that we mentioned earlier with the look-alike audiences. The conversion rates that you get with Facebook lookalike audiences (created using data together with machine intelligence) are sky-high in comparison with standard conversion rates. It would be interesting to compare the conversion rates from Facebook look-alike audiences to those that are obtained by throwing an ad up on a website like CNN.

Let's consider another social media website that we discussed in the last chapter: YouTube. YouTube is one of the busiest sites on the planet. Although it's not immediately obvious, you can use YouTube for rock bottom priced advertising in order to target people who have specific interests. All you have to do to advertise on YouTube is to create a simple video and then use that as the basis of an advertisement. Then you can state specifically where are you want that ad to show. You can even have them show it preceding the viewing of specific videos that you have identified. So, if you got a product to solve a certain need, you could have it advertised on videos that discussed a related issue. As an example, let's say that you sold a portable personal EKG machine. So, you can make a video demonstrating the machine to use as an advertisement. Next, have that ad placed just before videos about heart attacks and symptoms of heart attacks. As you can surmise, the people who are coming to view the video are already worried about having heart attacks. When they click to watch on the health video, your ad shows up, demonstrating the personal EKG machine for them to use. You can imagine how well that kind of targeted advertisement would convert!

YouTube is also a great site to utilize organic for free marketing. This does take a lot of time and effort, however. But if you're careful about the keywords you use in the video topics that you choose, making professionally looking videos over time, you will be able to build a following on YouTube and market to them. The key to good marketing videos on YouTube is to make the videos as if they were not marketing videos. You don't want to be explicitly marketing to people on YouTube. What you want to do on YouTube is to show people how to solve problems that are related to your business. This is like the approach when using a Facebook page. On the Facebook page, the apparent purpose of the page is to develop relationships with customers, not advertising to them - at least not very often. Building relationships with customers is something that's very effective because it creates a level of trust. Once people trust you, they are going to be easy to sell to and turn from prospects into customers of your business.

Customer Targeting

The amount of data that is available on social media is enormous. However, within the data, it is possible for companies to extract all kinds of information. You can learn things like education level, page likes, marital status, number of children, and what websites they visit.

This can have a lot of power when it comes to marketing. One of the key characteristics the social media provides is the ability of businesses to gain insight into customer demographics. This can be turned into actionable decisions by the business. This can include more effective targeted advertising, and the business can engage in active involvement with a potential customer base within the social media platform.

This offers an opportunity for the most efficient marketing and sales possible. First, a company can use Facebook or other social media companies in order to determine the demographics and interests of its customer base.

Search Engine Marketing

Another way that companies can use their online presence - together with large amounts of data - is through search engine marketing. You can use data that has been collected by companies like Microsoft and Google in order to laser target potential customers as they search on the Internet for topics related to your business. This type of marketing is powerful and inexpensive. Some of the data that you can utilize includes keywords from searches. Search engines will allow you to download data that includes keywords together with the number of searches that are done on each keyword. This helps determine which keywords are best to use in your own advertising.

Establishing an Internet Presence

Being everywhere is a critical component of your internet marketing efforts. This will involve new media and older media. By this, we mean that you should be on relevant social media platforms, providing real, relevant, and engaging content that helps you form relationships with customers. Second, you should have a blog. Many businesses miss the importance of a blog, not to mention the opportunity that exists for the collection of more data. Your blog should also engage prospects with timely, interesting, and relevant content that will help to expand your presence online. At the same time, you can collect data from readers while speaking to them directly. It can also be integrated with your Facebook page in order to create a feedback loop that can help power your online presence and marketing efforts.

Using Business Intelligence to Analyze and Improve

After you begin a large-scale Internet marketing approach, you will be able to turn your advertising and marketing data into inputs to business intelligence. This will allow you to convert raw data (about who responds to your marketing efforts) into reports and visualizations which can help management make data-driven decisions on future marketing efforts.

Another way to handle the data from Internet marketing is by feeding that data into machine learning systems. This is going to be useful to detect patterns, trends, and relationships in the data that can be used to gain actionable insights for the next round of your internet marketing efforts.

The key to a winning strategy with internet marketing is not to do more of the same. Instead, you should be continually collecting data from internet marketing efforts and feeding it to business intelligence, creating updated information and reports that can easily be absorbed and analyzed. The amount of data that is online is massive, and even in your own marketing efforts, you are going to be collecting colossal amounts of data that can seem to overwhelm. However, by using the right business intelligence process together with big data and machine learning, you are going to be able to turn that data into usable, actionable information that will take your marketing efforts to another level. This is going to be a continual feedback loop that will constantly be taking in enormous amounts of data and processing it in ways that can help your business refine its marketing efforts.

Identify Weak Spots

One of the most important uses of business intelligence with data collected from internet marketing is going to be identifying weak spots in your marketing plan. By processing, analyzing, and presenting data in a readable form, you will be able to find out what marketing efforts are not working and why. You will be able to update, refine, and improve your efforts and cycle through the process in order to get better results. When marketing efforts fail, you can kill the ones that don't work and put more effort into those that do. Each time you go through the cycle, you will achieve stronger and better internet marketing tactics that work to bring results.

Is internet marketing for everyone?

For some types of businesses, one question that arises is: should everyone be marketing online? The answer to this question is an absolute "YES!" The reason is simple: the data that can be collected is going to provide your business with new insights and actionable information. Even small "mom and pop" businesses would benefit from collecting and analyzing online data. Obviously, they are not going to have the infrastructure to do that themselves, but they can utilize services from companies like Facebook, gaining insights into their customer base and how they can better reach them. The companies that are constantly upgrading and updating are going to be the ones that will be able to achieve a competitive edge helping them achieve and maintain dominance in the marketplace.

Conclusion

Thank you for taking the time to read this book about business intelligence. If you did not know what business intelligence was before you started this book, it probably sounded like nothing more than another buzzword that has permeated corporate America. However, contained within the hype, business intelligence describes the kind of useful and important processes that businesses must adopt in order to stay competitive in this new technological and data-driven environment.

Business intelligence has been with us for some time. As soon as data was able to be gathered electronically and organized into the form of relational databases, businesses began developing procedures that would come to be later recognized as business intelligence. The advent of big data in machine learning is going to drive a revolution in business intelligence. Big data is completely changing the way that business intelligence is going to be used in the future. Big data represents a massive shift away from structured data in the form of relational databases and spreadsheets, and toward unstructured data that is being collected in massive amounts across all aspects of the business enterprise. Furthermore, big data can be used both for customer behavior and for the internal behavior of the employees of the company. Huge treasure troves of data have been collected on employee behavior, reflecting everything from emails, word processing documents, meeting notes, images, videos, and slideshow presentations. There are also huge amounts of data related to the use or misuse of resources within the company. One example of this involved Southwest Airlines trying to discover the reasons for – and costs of - leaving an idling aircraft on the tarmac. By using machine intelligence, the company was able to identify the problem and develop working solutions that were cost-effective, saving the company hundreds of millions of dollars in fuel costs. This example serves as a classic application of big data and machine intelligence for machine learning to business intelligence. Before we mentioned fuel savings, identification of the problem, and large cash savings by the business, you might not have identified machine learning as part of business intelligence. However, when we bring all these things together, it makes it clear that machine learning and big data have a direct application to the types of problems that are routinely solved using business intelligence.

Data has not only been available from internal sources collected by the company itself. In fact, data is being described as the new currency of business in the 21st century. As a result, many companies (including large ones like Facebook and Google) are using data itself in order to derive value for the company. This data can be shared with other corporations to drive the improvement of their own business intelligence.

As big data continues to be collected at a record pace and machine learning continues to improve and become more and more incorporated in business, it is incumbent upon corporations of all sizes to incorporate machine learning and big data into their strategy for business intelligence. Those companies able to do this successfully are the companies that are going to have a large competitive advantage in the marketplace. Those companies that are unable to do this (or that neglect to do it) are going to be the companies that are left behind. Thought processes must change when it comes to updating business intelligence. No longer can a company simply rely on the structured data that they have compiled into relational databases. As we mentioned earlier in the book, it is estimated that 90% of data that is now collected is in the form of unstructured data. Many companies are lost, not even sure how they can use this data or what they can do with it in a cost-effective manner.

As we go forward into the era of big data, cybersecurity is going to be increasingly important. Not only is it going to be important in a general sense, but cybersecurity is also going to play a larger and larger role in protecting business intelligence. Malicious actors are becoming much more emboldened as a business becomes more reliant on collecting and maintaining data. Therefore, although cybersecurity is not directly considered within business intelligence, it is going to play a supportive role that becomes more crucial as time goes on.

Many businesses have also been slow to adapt to the social media landscape. Over the past decade, social media has evolved from being a fringe activity of young people to becoming a centralized and crucially important component of the entire media landscape. Many issues are clouding the social media arena right now, including issues of privacy - which could have a large impact on the ways that businesses are able to share data amongst themselves. But one thing that we can be sure of: social media is here to stay. In one form or another, it will play a central role in communication and marketing in the future.

At this point, I would like to thank you for taking the time to read this book. I hope that you have found it informative and educational. If you have enjoyed the book, we certainly would appreciate it if you would leave us a review on Amazon. I would also like to encourage you to continue your education on the topics of big data, data science, machine intelligence, and business intelligence. Good luck in it all!

www.ingramcontent.com/pod-product-compliance
Lightning Source LLC
Chambersburg PA
CBHW050645190326
41458CB00008B/2425